D0424577

DIRT CHEAP
NYC

A HANGOVER MEDIA, INC. PUBLICATION
NEW YORK • NEW YORK

Published by
Shecky's
Hangover Media, Inc.
678 Broadway, 4th Fl.
New York, NY 10012

T: 212.242.2566
F: 212.242.3704
E: info@sheckys.com
www.sheckys.com

Written by: Jean Tang
Editor: Erin Donnelly
Layout Designer: Jennie Kim
Illustrators: Jennie Kim, Ginny Ligon
Editorial Assistants: Rebecca Krause, Jen Maxwell

Copyright 2005 by Hangover Media, Inc.
ISBN 1-931449-17-1

Printed in Canada

www.sheckys.com

I'm not one to make empty promises. Of course, you have only my word, but let me put it out there: This guidebook intends to make your fabulous NYC life more fun, more special, more interesting, more enriched…and much less costly.

Quite a claim, you say. Well, if you love your city as much as I do, you know at least a smidgen of what it offers in terms of personal enrichment (I'm not talking about enrichment in a financial sense, but if money's what popped into your head then at least you're on the right track). No other city in the world encompasses NYC's heady, combustible mix of arts, culture, nightlife, food, and ethnic diversity…along with $18 martinis, $100 theater tickets, $250 dates, and that ubiquitous, exorbitant rent. It's not just an urban drain—it's a suck. A suck-fest. Hear that noise? That's the scrape of my ATM card against the empty shell of my bank account.

Nope, this book does not target the destitute. The book costs money…and we're sure hoping you don't steal it. But I don't care what kind of salary you're living on. If you pay rent and are living an active urban life, you fall into a unique NYC category of destitution. The scrimp as you spend plan. The wear higher-heels-if-it'll-get-me-a-free-drink plan. A penny saved is one for the landlord. Or: A penny saved is one for a new pair of Manolo Blahniks. Which illustrates a nifty concept behind any kind of saving: The more you scrimp on one thing, the more you have to spend—or splurge—on another. There's only one kitty. Make the most of it.

WHY DIRT CHEAP NYC (THE LISTINGS) EXISTS

Dirt cheap events happen for a variety of reasons. For one

thing, we New Yorkers are extremely lucky, and private sponsors, donors, and charitable organizations give a lot of money to make sure the arts—visual arts, dance, music, drama—stay essential, even competitive. Barring for-profit ventures like privately owned galleries, most arts organizations channel revenue back into their cause, and thus are officially designated non-profit venues. This book will show you how you can spend a few hours at the Metropolitan Museum, catch a Saturday afternoon matinee, and then attend a play—all for $1.

On the other side of the public/private divide, take one of the oldest and simplest concepts known to man: a bar. You just got off work and you're tired, you're thirsty, and you're hungry. Of the thousands of NYC bars you can head for, which one are you going to pick? The one with the free chips and $2 beers? If you're on a budget, the answer's probably yes. All of the potential places—bar none (sorry, bad pun)—are out to score one thing: you…or more specifically, your hard-earned money. So they'd better pony up: better drinks, cheaper prices, free food. This book will guide you to the city's best happy hours.

Then there are the businesses that turn a steady buck by moving closeout merchandise. Even if you've never stepped foot in a Job Lot or a Liquidators, you've probably been the recipient of a closeout saving. What do you think supermarket specials are all about? This book will tell you how to have six friends over for fine wine and imported cheese—for about $6 a person.

WHY DIRT CHEAP NYC (THE BOOK) BEATS OTHERS ON THE MARKET

A word on those guides that came before. Some are exhaustive lists of venues and activities. That's not what you should expect here. First, it's not even a list: The descriptions of venues, events, services, merchandise, and advice are just that—descriptions, not the bare-bones facts. Secondly, this book is not exhaustive: The items included are all carefully screened—for quality, value, impact, content, consistency, and creativity. In other words, I'm not going to send you into a supermarket to pester the deli man for a bunch of thimble-sized samples. Sure, it'd be possible to get full that way, but where's the enjoyment in that?

WHAT DIRT CHEAP NYC (THE BOOK) DOES NOT INCLUDE

This is a book written by an adult for adults, so no kid stuff. Also note that the book is called "Shecky's DIRT CHEAP NYC: For Fun and Self-Improvement," so mundane necessities like health clinics and light bulbs are left out. You shouldn't be skimping on healthcare, anyhow.

Don't expect to see items you would ordinarily get for free, unless we considered them exceptional. Thus: gallery and public park—no; gallery opening, secret park—yes. Follow?

You also won't see anything obvious in here: fast food chains, for example, or busker performances in the subway. I'll trust you know enough to get yourself to a Mickey D's during $2 Big Mac season, and how to wolf down your burger while watching the Peruvian pipers do their thing in Times Square.

SOME OF THE THINGS DIRT CHEAP NYC (THE BOOK) INCLUDES

Do expect to see a thorough guide encompassing all five boroughs of the city, and, where appropriate, points in New Jersey, upstate New York, and Long Island.

Also, the value factor is based on relative cost. So I do include a $600 leather jacket that ordinarily costs $2,200, but not a happy hour where they take a measly $1 off of a $12 cocktail.

GETTING BY DIRT CHEAP NYC
(THE ACTUALITY)

This book can give you plenty of ideas on how to live a Dirt Cheap NYC life. The thing that it can't do is live it for you. For the kind of dirt cheap life that goes on and on and on, you have to do the hard work yourself.

Therefore do try this at home: Anytime you buy anything—be it a pair of pants, a gym membership, or a new sofa—think of it as an opportunity to hone your negotiating skills sharper than a butter knife under a slow flame. Keep your eyes peeled for sale signs blasting deals; the more you see, the more ammo you have as you approach your haggle target. And do haggle; do it with confidence and specificity (i.e., put your exact offer on the table). As with flirting, the art of haggling is an art that takes on a definitive gamesmanship over time.

No matter what propaganda Hollywood might spit your way, NYC is still the king of show business. The lights are brighter in Times Square, the sheer quantity of performances denser, the audiences laugh—and clap—harder, the guitars vibrate sweeter, the themes on and off Broadway resonate longer—and the performers hustle more (rent, baby!) for their art.

Obviously none of this has anything to do with the scions of renowned playwrights, rock bands, actors, opera singers, TV shows, and comedians for whom the Big Apple was a launching pad. Or the fact that we're as literary a city as we are passionate and diverse—and will turn out in the hundreds at the annual New Yorker Festival to watch Dave Eggers read from a snarky new collection of essays.

This chapter is the first of two in the book that shows you how to take advantage of the cauldron of talent seething right under your feet—and still have enough left over for an amazing meal (for which you should refer to Chapter 5). "Pop Cheap" spans rock and jazz, theater, films (along with their festivals and outdoor events), comedy, and finally the tube—live television. (In Chapter 3—Culture Cheap —we'll cover classical music, opera, and dance.)

So go to it. And Dave is smarter and funnier than Leno. He just is.

These days, rock 'n' roll is the broad title still used for a ridiculous array of music. Personally, I don't care; browse at will through this section and call the music whatever you like. The important thing is: The venues listed—a motley crew of bars, lounges, clubs, and listening rooms—charge you no to little cover for a great selection of live music.

ARLENE GROCERY
95 Stanton St. (Ludlow & Orchard Sts.)
Lower East Side 212.358.1633

This precious piece of real estate has gone from a family-owned grocery store with questionable produce, to a dank and seedy rock venue, to its current renovated digs as home to a slew of different things. Rock is king: The performances are engaging, and not just because they're loud. For $7 or less, you get to see a whole lineup of bands. Aside from great acoustics, the band room has its own bar and a stage that won't cause you to crane your neck. The comfortable bar area adjacent has a cluster of tall tables and chairs, and the back room is lined with wooden banquettes, low tables, and small, ass-numbing stools. And yes, Monday night's free punk/metal karaoke is as freaky as it sounds—and has a following bigger than Marilyn Manson's makeup collection. I promise you'll remember the night long after the temporary hearing loss has worn off.

BARBES

376 9th St. (@ 6th Ave.)
Park Slope 718.965.9177

Give two French musicians a 1,000-square-foot venue with a cozy back room, and voila! What comes out the other end is a world music venue in its own happy tradition. This South Slope bar and lounge fills a performance gap in this friendly Brooklyn neighborhood. (Proof positive: During Blackout 2003, hundreds of disoriented Slopees gathered here to drink.) The unusual name, derived from a Parisian neighborhood with a large North African population, ensures that the evenings become eclectic: Performances have ranged from Algerian diva Asmahan to Mexican bandas, from Venezuelan joropos to Romanian brass bands, to the crazy, surreal ukulele/chord organ/viola/upright bass/drums/vocal combo called Songs from a Random House. Count on popular repeat performances by One Ring Zero, a recorded local band, and bluegrass artists Johnny Staats and Robert Shafer. The Barbes policy is generally no cover, but top acts might run you $5-$10.

CBGB's

315 Bowery (1st & 2nd Sts.)
East Village 212.982.4052

To say you played here puts your band up there with The Police, Blondie, and The Ramones. Never mind that the "home of underground rock" is a dive with a greasy capital "D"—this historical badge of honor is still part of the quintessential New York music scene. The cutesy name stands for "country bluegrass blues," but founder-owner Hilly Kristal's intentions were foiled—in a good way—when punk and rock literally showed up on his doorstep. Kudos to CBGB's for surviving the Bowery back when it was lined with alcoholic derelicts (there used to be a flophouse upstairs). Hats off to tradition: Most nights, it's $7 to get in (weekends are $10). Come Monday, it's your turn to be the judge: $3 gets you through the door at 6:30pm to watch a completely hit-or-miss lineup of rock star wannabes audition. Expect to see a little sucking.

CODA
34 E. 34th St. (@ Madison Ave.)
Midtown 212.685.3434

Don't let the ol' velvet rope/bouncer routine keep you away from this live music lounge. Coda doesn't have that snobbish attitude you'd expect from a swanky spot with a Murray Hill address. At first glance, you'd never know a bank once occupied this large, high-ceilinged space, but venture downstairs to "the vault" and you're sure to be clued in—the safety deposit boxes lining the wall of the retro-furnished loft inspire naughty make-out fantasies. Featuring a two-band lineup most weekday nights, you'll hear anything from jazz to rock, all in an upscale yet comfortable atmosphere (covers range from free to $10). Slip onto a cushy cranberry couch and nibble on trendy appetizers like the cheese and chocolate fondues. Wash it all down with one of Coda's sweet drink concoctions like Whole Lotta Love or Tush (try ordering that one without blushing). Cool music, cool crowd, no cover—sounds like some good reasons to get in tune with Coda.

DON HILL'S
511 Greenwich St. (@ Spring St.)
SoHo 212.219.2850

For a measly $10, Don Hill's has something for everyone. Whether it's '80s retro DJs, live local bands, dance parties, or heavy metal night, this big, dark, boxy space knows how to throw a party. The décor, or lack thereof, is minimal at best, but how do you decorate for a theme night that changes dramatically every 24 hours? For the love of God, please call ahead for a schedule—if you show up in your spiked leather head-banging gear on transvestite night, you may be in for more than you can handle, toughie.

GALAPAGOS ART SPACE
70 N. 6th St. (Kent & Wythe Aves.)
Williamsburg 718.782.5188

You might think a Zen reflecting pool has no business in a rock venue—until you lay eyes on the one at Galapagos. Housed in a former mayonnaise factory, Galapagos has won awards for its stunning design: Unlike the black box you're used to, there's light in here, and air, and angles to gaze at, and a wondrous, soaring ceiling. There's plenty happening: free dancing and DJs on Thursdays, Fridays, and Saturdays, and live music on Saturday nights for a mere $5 cover (before 11pm; after 11pm it's free to get in). Check out Amateur Night on Tuesdays. It's rare for a cover charge here to exceed $5.

THE LIVING ROOM
154 Ludlow St. (Stanton & Rivington Sts.)
Lower East Side 212.533.7237

Vive la difference! When the new Living Room opened its doors in the fall of 2003, we drew no link between the old location's distressed cobweb look and the new one's glowing-orange aura. Then the music played, and we said, "Aha." Known for singer/songwriter-based music from the substantial local talent pool (making this more listening room, less rock club), this is one of the most undemanding venues to catch a few foot-thumping tunes. By undemanding, I mean of you. There is rarely a cover or an enforcement of the one-drink minimum, you'll have lots of room to stand, sit, or lean, and there's no requirement to commit to a performance for any period of time. A donation bucket collects bills for the players. Dish it up, as the performances are good—if it's any indication, Norah Jones has been known to drop in (in rare instances you may need to buy a $20 ticket to see a Duncan Sheik). Check out BMI Night on the last Wednesday of every month, in which the publishing company sends out its young lyricists—great musicians in their own right—for some local exposure. The new location has a mellow, upstairs lounge where on some nights, guest DJs will weave a spell with their records.

LUNA LOUNGE
171 Ludlow St. (Houston & Stanton Sts.)
Lower East Side 212.260.2323

Luna Lounge is an excellent place to see free music without having to deal with the hipster arrogance that clouds many similar music venues. The first room is for hanging, drinking, and playing foosball. The back room features up-and-coming bands, usually of the punk or rock variety that often pack the place tighter than a trannie in a truss, sometimes even spilling fans into the bar area to watch the act on the TV above the bar. The closest thing to The Strokes will be in the jukebox, but for the most part the bands are worth the risk. Beers are $3 and up, and you can find all sorts of interesting people looking to pound their eardrums with something more inter-esting than techno, hip-hop, or that oh-so-dreadful electro-clash.

MANITOBA'S
99 Ave. B (6th & 7th Sts.)
East Village 212.982.2511

Bikers, heavy metal, and the art of goth are still alive in Alphabet City at Manitoba's. A tattoo motif covers the walls, accompanied by various posters for live shows by '70s bands like The Ramones and Sex Pistols that look like they've been there since 1983. The bartender is cynical and surly, the music free, and the drinks quick and dirty. Rock 'n' roll rules here, so if you're not wearing your black leather zippered jacket, there might be a problem.

MERCURY LOUNGE
217 E. Houston St. (@ Ave. A)
Lower East Side 212.260.4700

The Mercury Lounge isn't alien, but it is out of this world, with a solid talent roster and a space to match. Divided between the bar room and the band room, Mercury is both a place to hang, have a drink, and see a band…or keep the drink and scrap the band, your pick. General cover ranges from $8-$10. The spacious band room is packed nightly with fans of every genre screaming their guts out for the up and coming and those who are already up and ready to rock your world. And remember to bring your ID; they're serious about that here.

PADDY REILLY'S
519 2nd Ave. (@ 29th St.)
Murray Hill 212.686.1210

Paddy Reilly's is just about the most original Dublin pub to hit the United States in some time. Eight taps spell out the only thing they sell by the pint: Guinness (if you want some diversity, they've got a special extra-cold Guinness machine available…then some other imported and domestic beers by the bottle). With the help of a 24/7 webcam, Paddy Reilly's is known far and wide for its devotion to free live music. You name it, if it relates to the Irish, it's here: traditional Irish, random folk, Celtic rock, performers like the Prodigals and Tom Hanway, and the popular Bluegrass Sunday night. The crowd ranges from local to international, and all everyone seems to have in common is their penchant for good beer, good music, and enjoying both long past their bedtimes.

PARKSIDE LOUNGE
317 E. Houston St. (Aves. B & C)
Lower East Side 212.673.6270

If you are looking for the trendsetters and added cool, then you're in the wrong place as the crowd here is actually normal. An excellent place to hang out after work or on the weekends, it is far enough away from the trendy bars that you shouldn't have to worry about hurting yourself on an over-starched i-banker's oxford shirt and the only labels you'll see will be on your beer. Fridays are for salsa, Saturdays for comedy and rock 'n' roll, Mondays for bluegrass—the live musical acts usually end in some drunken dancing (cover's anywhere from free to $5). Tuesdays see an open mike comedy night (see Laugh Cheap). Cheap and fun, grab a pool cue and feel free to miss every shot. It's just that kind of place.

PETE'S CANDY STORE
709 Lorimer St. (Richardson & Frost Sts.)
Williamsburg 718.302.3770

A free music joint with cheap, original cocktails ($7), and cheaper, yummy sandwiches (try the fresh mozzarella and pesto on ciabatta) is the kind of Manhattan fantasy that comes true in Williamsburg. What's more, Pete's—a former candy store—has elbow room to spare, even on bustling weekend nights. Music at Pete's leans towards folky, and the relaxed vibe provided by smooth music extends from the cozy front bar space to the room with the stage, the side vestibule (in which pew-like benches provide additional seating), and a large Christmas-lit back patio. Early in the evening, Pete's doubles as a game parlor, and on warm Sundays, it's backyard barbeque time. Respect for the neighborhood keeps the noise level down.

SIBERIA
356 W. 40th St. (8th & 9th Aves.)
Hell's Kitchen 212.333.4141

When the Mitsubishi Company wasn't willing to renew the lease on the old subway bar at 50th Street, the owner of Siberia took extreme measures, flying to Tokyo to insist with a toilet bowl chained to his leg. It didn't work, but Siberia—now known as the former subway bar—landed in a nice enough spot. The lofty ceilings and the two floors still make the free lounge seem roomy even on a Friday night. The live music is still good, and not even the fixtures have gone anywhere: The Ms. Pac-Man game, the Addams Family pinball machine, and the original '50s photo booth are still there, as are the skanky couches. Thanks to the stubborn owner, door rules remain the same: There's to be no cussing and no hitting on women. The exposed brick and plaster walls are slowly filling with graffiti and pictures, so bring a memento to tack to the wall before the Russian icons take up all the available space in this landmark to be. A rare dive still in its glory days—pass by and leave your mark.

SOUTHPAW
125 5th Ave. (Sterling Pl. & St. John's Pl.)
Park Slope 718.230.0236

Park Slopers who have given up on the Mercury Lounge due to an acute case of F-trainaphobia are fortunate to have Southpaw. This former 99-cent store has been prettied up beyond all recognition by two Brooklyn buddies, who gutted it and started completely anew. This is a great date spot; the seats are cushioned and the tables intimate, and the record covers stapled to the wall are pristine enough to read. Nightly, up-and-coming cutting-edge bands like Mogwai and The Trachtenburg Family Slideshow Players play punk, new wave, hip-hop, electronica, and old-time rockers like The Fleshtones play here as well. Tickets ($5-$20) are available through www.ticketweb.com and at the door.

TERRA BLUES
149 Bleecker St. (Thompson St. & LaGuardia Pl.) West Village 212.777.7776

Warm fuzzies come over you as soon as you walk off of loud and chaotic Bleecker Street and into this classic blues nightspot. The black arched ceiling and walls are accented by subtle red lights, flickering candles, and vague white figures that swell from the walls. But stop staring at the décor because you're here for the blues, and the blues you will get. Magic Slim, blues artist of 2003, comes from the Windy City once or twice a year, and it's only a ten-spot to catch his act. That's the most you will pay here; usually it's more like $5-$10 for mind-blowing acoustic sets that are certain to impress even the most hardcore music aficionado.

TONIC
107 Norfolk St. (Delancey & Rivington Sts.) Lower East Side 212.358.7501

This quirky, incongruous, free-standing building on a quiet block of Norfolk Street looks like something you'd see in L.A., not the Lower East Side. It bills itself as a haven for avant-garde, creative, and experimental jazz/rock/electronic music, and rightfully so. Tonic has made its name as a mecca for music lovers with some of the most innovative live acts around, and its tiny, pleasant space makes it an unusually comfortable venue for live shows. The cellar-like basement bar offers realistically priced drinks and gets crammed with arty downtown and Williamsburg types pre- and post-show. (You'll hear some decidedly free-form sounds down here as well.) Cover charges depend on who's playing, but $12 is usually the top ticket price. It is an old-fashioned tonic for big city blues.

Who knows why jazz isn't as popular as its rockin' counterpart? To me, there is nothing that can conjure a NYC atmosphere more instantaneously than the velvet vibes of a saxophone under some madly evocative lighting. Check out the following clubs and other venues for very modestly priced shows, concerts, and jam sessions.

THE BLUE NOTE
131 W. 3rd St. (MacDougal St. & 6th Ave.)
Greenwich Village 212.475.8592

Ordinarily, this place ain't cheap: I once paid $75 to see Oscar Peterson in his post-stroke comeback concert. With a $5 per person minimum on top of the cover (typically $25-$35), you and your date will be spending the New York median: a few hundred bucks. But on Monday nights, when lesser-known artists pop up on the tiny stage, the cover goes down…way down. Call ahead for exceptions, but it's generally $10 for both the 8pm and 10:30pm shows ($5 off if you sit at the bar at either show or flash a student ID at the later show). The bar's more remote than the tables, but here's the drawback with the tables: You're seated by staff with a 50-50 chance of sitting with your back to whoever's playing. Better like that date of yours.

THE CAJUN
129 8th Ave. (@ 16th St.)
Chelsea 212.691.6174

If Dixieland is what you want, you'll settle for no less than The

Cajun, which bills itself as the taste and sound of New Orleans. Step inside for live nightly shows (there's a noon show on Wednesdays and Sundays), including The Red Onion Jazz Band and Stan Rubin's Swing Era Band. There's no cover or drink minimum, but you must order a dinner entrée while you enjoy the show.

CLEOPATRA'S NEEDLE
2485 Broadway (92nd & 93rd Sts.)
Upper West Side 212.769.6969

This is our kind of spot: live jazz every night of the week, zero cover, and a low, $10 per person minimum at tables, where you can order big portions of Mediterranean food, $5 bottled beer, and $8 cocktails. The nightly shows start at 8pm, followed by an after-hours jam session most nights for people who never, ever want to go to sleep. Sunday afternoons, it's an open mic from 2pm-6pm. You might get lucky: Wynton Marsalis and Roy Hargrove have both dropped by.

DETOUR
349 E. 13th St. (1st & 2nd Aves.)
East Village 212.533.6212

Tucked away on an unassuming block in the East Village, friendly and casual Detour brings two good things together in one low-key space: live jazz seven nights a week and no cover. Yes, there's a catch: You've got to knock down two drinks during the show. Listen up though: Claim a hangover from the night before, and see the rule magically go away (even if your real-live headache doesn't). Most nights, the live music starts at 9pm; come early, and you can typically get a table for two. Bonus: Arrivals before 7pm score choice picks on the jukebox and happy hour for $3 pints, bottles, and mixed drinks.

THE JUILLIARD SCHOOL OF MUSIC
65th St. (Broadway & Amsterdam Ave.)
Upper West Side 212.769.7406

Classical music makes up the lion's share of the free and paid events at this conservatory, but the recent two- and four-year jazz programs mean that fans of looser forms don't get short shrift. Twice yearly, the Juilliard Jazz Ensembles and Jazz Orchestra get to take over the stage at Alice Tully Hall. Although the performances are free, you still have to pick up tickets two weeks prior at the Juilliard box office. Call ahead.

SMOKE
2751 Broadway (105th & 106th Sts.)
Upper West Side 212.864.6662

When the smaller-name acts are booked (typically weekdays), this plush club—now smoky only in spirit—lets you in for the price of a measly $10 drink minimum. The velvety drapes and sofas soften the music, causing it to drift over like so much smoke. Actually, the club was named after Paul Auster's novel, which he wrote on the premises back when the club was known as Augie's. There are as many as three sets a night, sometimes with lively jam sessions running 'til the wee hours.

ST. NICK'S PUB
773 St. Nicholas Ave. (@ 149th St.)
Harlem 212.283.9728

Spirited Monday night jam sessions can spark up the beginning of your dreary weeks. With a $3 cover, the Sugar Hill Jazz Quartet—led by saxist Patience Higgins—is now world-famous, thanks to busloads of tourists who arrive, cameras and all, at the start of the sessions. But don't let that stop you from making the trek to Harlem: James Carter, Reggie Workman, and all the up-and-coming artists on their way to commandeering acts at bigger, Midtown venues have all dropped in on the open mike. The only catch is a two-drink minimum. Beers are $5 (bottles; no drafts), and cocktails $8. Take a cue from Ella and get on that 'A' train to go to Sugar Hill way up in Harlem.

ZINC BAR
90 W. Houston St. (@ LaGuardia Pl.)
Greenwich Village 212.477.8337

This jazz club is exactly what one should be: dim and mysterious, like a mini satanic secret. The aura of hidden-ness touches everything: the exposed-brick walls, the close-fitting seats, even the staircase leading to the entrance. The spot would be perfect with a date: making out to the groovy tunes in these tucked-away environs can hardly be considered PDA. For $5, sink into the live sounds of jazz, Brazilian, and African music. There is a drink minimum, but rest assured: You're not going to get some watered-down excuse for a drink. The mojitos are some of the best in the city and the homemade sangria is nearly hallucinatory.

The lights go down, the curtain goes up, and a silence wraps its long arms around a sold-out house. OK, it's not always sold out—but when it is, you're probably in for a great performance. There's a lot of theater in NYC, not all of it good and certainly not all of it free. This section is intended to help you make some wise picks while getting your tickets for free or extremely cheap.

AUDIENCE EXTRAS
Various theaters 212.686.1966

Everyone knows about TKTS, where the lines drag and the suspense of not knowing what you're going to see bites. But here's a cheaper alternative, where the surprise factor doesn't leave you scrambling for your wallet on 42nd Street. Audience Extras was founded by a New York playwright and producer to make theater affordable for NYC residents, all while serving an important function for the art. Like the name implies, the "club" provides extras to fill the audience (for previews or critic-attended performances). In industry parlance it's known as papering the house; for you it means a dicey but interesting mix of off-Broadway, comedy, and experimental productions for an $85 membership fee, and then an additional $3 for each ticket (up to two) that you order. In exchange, you have to maintain a super-discreet vibe; the company—which assumes that any linked show will acquire a stigma—wants you to keep them hush-hush.

THE BEST, NO-RUSH, OFF-BROADWAY STUDENT TICKETS

If you've got a hankering for good, inexpensive theater, your pickings will be far easier at the smaller, so-called off-Broadway venues (the designation's a product of house take as much as geography) than on the broad strip itself. If you're a currently enrolled student with a picture ID, the pickings get even better. Typically, theaters will sell any available tickets to students an hour before the performance (ergo, the rush).

There are legions of worthy companies out there, but the one that delivers the best value for student money is Second Stage Theater (also see ushering section). The student subscription deal is unbeatable, at $60 for four top-notch plays. If you're still enrolled, it gets even better after year one, with a $40 renewal fee, or $10 per play—no rush required.

Then again, if you haven't graduated yet and you're into rushing, so be it. Here are some other good companies:

45 Bleecker ($21 student rush tickets, also see ushering section) has staged the critically acclaimed one-woman show, *Bridge & Tunnel*, and *The Exonerated*, which brought to life the playwrights' interviews with wrongly accused inmates on death row.

Manhattan Theater Club ($20 student rush tickets, also see ushering section) features brand-new productions on its two stages. You're likely to see a celebrity: Sarah Jessica Parker and Mary Tyler Moore—icons of their respective generations—have each performed here. The rules are a little different here: arrive two hours before the performance, and buy up to four tickets per valid student ID.

If you're a theater geek and like a headier performance, check out the Signature Theatre Company ($15 student rush tickets, also see ushering section), which dedicates entire seasons to a single living American playwright. The scribe gets ensconced in the productions.

Playwrights Horizons ($15 student rush tickets, also see ushering section) has an eye for debuting solid new productions, including *Recent Tragic Events*, which opened with Heather Graham in a comedy that takes place on 9/12/01.

45 BLEECKER
45 Bleecker St. (@ Lafayette St.)
NoHo 212.253.9983

MANHATTAN THEATER CLUB
131 W. 55th St. (6th & 7th Aves.)
Midtown 212.581.1212

PLAYWRIGHTS HORIZONS
416 W. 42nd St. (9th & 10th Aves.)
Hell's Kitchen 212.564.1235

SECOND STAGE THEATER
307 W. 43rd St. (@ 8th Ave.)
Midtown 212.246.4422

SIGNATURE THEATRE COMPANY
555 W. 42nd St. (10th & 11th Aves.)
Hell's Kitchen 212.244.7529

PLAYING ON THE FRINGE

Various venues in downtown Manhattan
212.279.4488

It started the way so much starts in New York—from a point of passion. Some theater-loving friends were too poor to take a play they'd produced to Edinburgh, Scotland, where the original Fringe Festival occurs. Someone suggested New York needed its own Fringe. The idea became a rumbling; then the rumbling gathered momentum until pretty soon, by golly, New York had its very own festival, now going on seven years. OK, so maybe you don't think paying $15 for an off-off-off-Broadway play is money well spent. But would you rather pay $80 to see the likes of *Urinetown* or *Debbie Does Dallas*? It's clearly not impossible to strike gold; the thing to do is to pore over the early reviews. (The festival is too important now for any of the New York rags to disregard.) Then decide what you want to see. True, some of the festival's 20-plus downtown venues (i.e. the Village's Independent Theater, which seats less than 30) are teensy-tiny, but if you plan carefully (arrive early, come on a weekday afternoon), you'll get in. And then brag that you saw it here first.

FOR THE PRICE OF A SMILE

If the word "usher" gives you a flashback to high school, when you worked at the local multiplex picking up popcorn after the same kids who made fun of your velour sweatpants in gym class, well, go see a therapist. For everyone else, this is one heck of a way to get into some of the city's best shows and meet some other passionate (or cheapo) theater people. And it involves way less than you probably think.

First, pick a show that you want to see. Let your frugal imagination go wild—most off-Broadway theaters and dance venues make use of the free help—see the list below. Next, call ahead to reserve a spot, or a couple (take note, single men with dollar signs painted to the back of your eyeballs...you know who you are). This might be a few weeks out depending on the popularity of the show.

On the day, you show up an hour before curtain time wearing specified clothing (usually all-black, white and black, or just conservative clothes). The house manager will give you a debriefing and rundown of the house. Light duties follow—no, vacuuming is generally not on the list; it's more like stuffing inserts into fliers, propping doors open, and cordoning off restricted areas. When it comes time to seat people, smile big and try to refrain from saying, "You paid for your ticket, sucker!" to their face. Then—for the most part—your work is finito. Sometimes you can snag an open seat; sometimes ushers have chairs. Sometimes you have to stand, but hey, if that's the case, you can hardly complain that big hair blocked your view of the show.

Venues:

ASTOR PLACE THEATRE
434 Lafayette St. (E. 4th & E. 8th Sts.)
East Village 212.254.4370

ATLANTIC THEATER COMPANY
336 W. 20th St. (8th & 9th Aves.)
Chelsea 212.645.8015

CENTURY CENTER THEATER
111 E. 15th St. (Union Sq. East & Irving Pl.)
Gramercy 212.982.6782 ext. 11

THE CHERRY LANE THEATRE
38 Commerce St. (Bedford & Hudson Sts.)
West Village 212.989.2020

CITY CENTER'S ENCORE SERIES
130 W. 56th St. (6th & 7th Aves.)
Midtown 212.247.0430 ext. 202

CLASSIC STAGE COMPANY
136 E. 13th St. (3rd & 4th Aves.)
East Village 212.677.4210 ext. 30

ENSEMBLE STUDIO THEATRE
549 W. 52nd St. (10th & 11th Aves.)
Hell's Kitchen 212.247.4982

45 Bleecker Theater and Gallery
45 Bleecker St. (Bowery & Lafayette St.)
NoHo 212.253.7017

Irish Arts Center
553 W. 51st St. (10th & 11th Aves.)
Hell's Kitchen 212.757.3318

Irish Repertory Theatre
132 W. 22nd St. (6th & 7th Aves.)
Chelsea 212.255.0270

Jean Cocteau Repertory Theater
330 Bowery (@ 2nd St.)
East Village 212.677.0060 ext. 16

John Houseman Theater
450 W. 42nd St. (9th & 10th Aves.)
Hell's Kitchen 212.967.7079

Lucille Lortel Foundation
121 Christopher St. (Hudson & Bleecker
Sts.) West Village 212.924.2817

Manhattan Ensemble Theater
55 Mercer St. (Broome & Grand Sts.)
SoHo 212.925.1900

Manhattan Theatre Club
at the City Center
W. 55th St. (6th & 7th Aves.)
Hell's Kitchen 212.247.0430 ext. 240

Mint Theater Company
311 W. 43rd St., 5th Fl. (8th & 9th Aves.)
Hell's Kitchen 212.315.9434

NEW YORK THEATRE WORKSHOP
79 E. 4th St. (2nd Ave. & Bowery)
East Village 212.780.9037

**THE PEARL THEATRE COMPANY
AT THEATRE 80**
80 St. Marks Pl. (1st & 2nd Aves.)
East Village 212.598.9802

THE PERFORMING GARAGE
33 Wooster St. (Broome & Grand Sts.)
SoHo 212.966.3651

PLAYHOUSE 91
316 E. 91st St. (1st & 2nd Aves.)
Upper East Side 212.831.20001

PLAYWRIGHTS HORIZONS
416 W. 42nd St. (9th & 10th Aves.)
Hell's Kitchen 212.564.1235

P.S. 122
150 1st Ave. (@ E. 9th St.)
East Village 212.477.5829 ext. 306

THE ROUNDABOUT THEATRE COMPANY
The American Airlines Theater
227 W. 42nd St. (7th & 8th Aves.)
Midtown 212.719.9393

SECOND STAGE THEATRE
307 W. 43rd St. (@ 8th Ave.)
Hell's Kitchen 212.246.4422

THE SIGNATURE THEATRE COMPANY
555 W. 42nd St. (10th & 11th Aves.)
Hell's Kitchen 212.244.7529

THE VINEYARD THEATRE
108 E. 15th St. (Union Sq. East & Irving Pl.)
Gramercy 212.353.3366 ext. 226

WOMEN'S PROJECT THEATRE
424 W. 55th St. (9th & 10th Aves.)
Hell's Kitchen 212.765.1706

YORK THEATRE COMPANY
619 Lexington Ave. (@ 54th St.)
Midtown 212.935.5824 ext. 19

THE JUILLIARD SCHOOL OF MUSIC
65th St. (Broadway & Amsterdam Ave.)
Upper West Side 212.769.7406

Think Juilliard and think classical music, but a handful of free plays which undergo public workshops in the drama theater do the school proud. Also, the Spring Dance Concert inhabits the Juilliard Theater in a flurry of anticipation amongst the cherry blossoms: The week's span of performances isn't free, but surely you can pony up $15 to gaze at the handsome men in tights. Call ahead to confirm availability for both events.

NEW YORK CITY BALLET
New York State Theater (63rd St., West of Broadway) Upper West Side 212.870.5570

The Fourth Ring Society sounds like a Tolkien inspired fan club. But it's a glorified phrase for nosebleed, which in turn is synonymous with sticking your tongue out at the antlike people below and telling those suckers that you got in for practically free. I have three words for them: cheap plastic binoculars.

The populist City Ballet—best known for annual productions of *The Nutcracker*—ordinarily costs $32-$70 for a ticket. But your $15 society membership fee covers you for winter and spring repertory performances (a mix of ballets, no *Nutcracker*, unfortunately). Then you pay a lousy $12—just a little more than a movie ticket—for each of up to two tickets per performance to watch the pretty pas de deux from the highest tier of the 2,700-seat New York State Theater. As a bonus, you get to attend dance discussions held before select performances—think of it as the "making of" section of a DVD. Just don't drool on anyone downstairs.

PROFESSIONAL PERFORMING ARTS HIGH SCHOOL
328 W. 48th St. (8th & 9th Aves.)
Midtown 212.247.8652

PPAS is not to be confused with the school made famous in *Fame*. But it may as well be—that school is now defunct, and the quality and caliber of the 6th through 12th grade instruction given here is nothing to shake a pointed foot at. During the school year, you only get two chances to watch these hard-working students in action—for the winter play (November or December), and the spring musical (April). Better hustle for your $10 ticket: The 700-seat auditorium usually sells out.

SHAKESPEARE IN CENTRAL PARK
Delacorte Theater (Mid-Park @ 80th St.)
Central Park

God bless benefactors. Through their support and generosity, we New Yorkers get a wowser of a non-profit organization: the fabulous, historic, highly regarded Public Theater. Founded by Joseph Papp—cultural altruist homeboy—as a Shakespeare workshop in 1954, the Public Theater has some age-old traditions the city couldn't do without. The first—and possibly best—of these is summer's Shakespeare in Central Park, held in the Public Theater's summer home, the Delacorte, a sweeping, outdoor amphitheater in the midst of our favorite warm-weather playground.

What's the catch, say you, ever the cynic. Just one: It takes work to score a pair of free tickets that are distributed outside the Public every day (see sidebar). But it's worthwhile; the twilight shows are typically phenomenal, and the fact that they're free does not lead to skimping on any production detail—and certainly not the quality and renown of the actors involved. In the recent past, the Shakespeare series—which doesn't necessarily confine itself to Shakespeare plays—has featured Chekhov's *The Seagull* starring icon Meryl Streep, along with Kevin Kline, Christopher Walken, and Natalie Portman, and *Henry V* starring Liev Schreiber. The plays—which start at 8pm—run long, so plan on eating early, or else being at the mercy of the concession stand (although since you got in for free, you can probably afford $6 for a sandwich).

TIP: Bring some bug spray: It gets buggy out there.

THE LINE

On play days beginning at around 10am, a line forms outside the Public Theater's permanent year-round home on Lafayette Street. Tickets are given out at 1pm, so the real early birds have a few hours to kill. A line monitor in a ranger hat is there to instruct these patient souls about the rules of the line: two tickets per person, a total half-hour break, no saving of spots for friends. It tends to be a happy crowd of people—young and old—reading, chatting gaily to friends and on cell phones, some even throwing their jackets down for a makeshift picnic. (Cheerfulness indicator: how willingly people accept unsolicited flyers; in a line last summer, I heard several line-goers chat with the pamphlet-givers.)

Tip: You're in the great outdoors, so bring an umbrella if it looks like rain.

HOT TICKET, STUDENT RUSH

This hot NYC dance company only performs a few times a year in its own hometown, so when performances happen, be sure to catch them. The company—whose members root their sensual, often modern and often exotic moves in classic ballet—sometimes gives free performances at Lincoln Center Out of Doors in the summertime. Otherwise, student rush tickets are $10, available between noon and 6pm on the day of performances during the December-long New York tour.

ALVIN AILEY AMERICAN DANCE CENTER
(@ City Center)
130 W. 56th St. (6th & 7th Aves.)
Midtown 212.767.0590

Fill in the blank with some big city indignation (got a demotion, apartment was burgled for the second time in three months, had your foot stomped in the subway). Apply comedy, press hard, repeat. For the remedy to work, you don't have to pay the outrageous cover charges at comedy clubs (offenders are usually uptown).

THE GERSHWIN
7 E. 27th St. (@ 5th Ave.)
Gramercy 212.545.8000

It's only $5 to get into the poorly named 10:17 Comedy Night, which takes place Saturdays at 9pm. But whatever…you get two endearing hosts, you get variety acts, you get sketch, you get silly musical revues, and most importantly, you get laughter. Thursdays and Fridays are also funny time at this hotel, which doubles as a Pop Art museum, replete with Warhol.

LUNA LOUNGE
171 Ludlow St. (Houston & Stanton Sts.)
Lower East Side 212.260.2323

Luna Lounge marks the return of stand-up to its performance room in the rear of the club. On Monday nights, $8 will buy you the show and a drink. Luna's got one of the most casual vibes in the city. Afterwards, you can hang out in the room with the bar and one of the city's few foosball tables.

PARKSIDE LOUNGE
317 E. Houston St. (Aves. B & C)
Lower East Side 212.673.6270

If you are looking for the trendsetters and added cool, then you're in the wrong place, as the crowd here is actually normal. An excellent place to hang out after work or on the weekends, it is far enough away from the trendy bars that you shouldn't have to worry about hurting yourself on an over-starched i-banker's oxford shirt and the only labels you'll see will be on your beer. Tuesdays see an open mic comedy night which is $7 to perform (but you get a free drink) and a two-drink minimum ($2-$7 per drink) to watch.

UPRIGHT CITIZEN'S BRIGADE
307 W. 26th St. (@ 8th Ave.)
Chelsea 212.366.9176

Here's one truly for the masses. The four owner-performers of this venue had a vision so counterintuitive as to be revolutionary—a populist theater that would offer the funniest comedy for the lowest prices. Proletariats everywhere will be happy to know about the astonishing success of their mission. The nightly improv and sketch shows are irreverent, creative, and generally sidesplitting. Tickets run anywhere from free to $8. (You'd need to get your head checked if you'd rather go to Caroline's and spend $35/person, plus a two-drink minimum.) There is no drink minimum; in fact, although you can buy soft drinks, there isn't even really a bar. And those other clubs can't even pull the fame card: Performers from here have gone on to write for Conan O'Brien, *The Daily Show* with Jon Stewart, and *Saturday Night Live* (Tina Fey, Horatio Sanz, and UCB co-owner Amy Poehler are all *SNL* regulars). The UCB theater's new location—double the size of the one down the street—is sort of a theater-in-the-semi-round. Note: Free shows are Wednesday's "Hump Night" and Sunday's

"Asssscat," when the owners and other notable alumni perform a weekly improv show that costs $8 at 7:30pm and is free at 9:30pm (come at 8pm to take a number).

The country's best television tapings happen here, usually in Midtown and almost always to sellout crowds with an audience strewn with out-of-towners. What gives? The combined result of procrastination and other life happenings has allowed hordes of Midwesterners to replace us in some of the city's best entertainment. Stop the outrage. Claim your spot!

The level of commitment to attend does depend on the show. A hot ticket like *Saturday Night Live*, for example, will take up to a year's wait to find out if you've won in an annual lottery—then within two weeks, you'll have to clear your calendar on the requisite Saturday. On the other end of the spectrum, you could line up for a standby spot on *The Late Show with David Letterman*, or make a phone call about a week in advance to see the newer, lesser-known *Last Call with Carson Daly*.

TIP 1: Studios uniformly pump in refrigerated air for the heat-sensitive cameras, so the rooms are kept brisk. Dress appropriately.

TIP 2: When it comes time to be seated, smile hard. If your enthusiasm shows, you are more likely to get a seat closer to the camera…and the action.

THE DAILY SHOW WITH JON STEWART
Comedy Central
1775 Broadway (57th & 58th Sts.)
Midtown 212.767.8600

Leave a message on the cancellation hotline that allows you to avoid the other unavoidable: a long waitlist to get on this popular show. Show coordinators will call you back.

EMERIL LIVE
Food Network Studios
604 W. 52nd St. (11th Ave. & West Side Hwy.)
Hell's Kitchen 212.398.8836

Yes, his constant "BAM!" is annoying. And yes, with the continuous rotation of his two shows on the network, he is a tad overexposed. But that's not to say we couldn't all learn a lifetime recipe or two from the fuzzy little chef from Louisiana. So as long as you're tuning in, why not go straight to the source?

Even with all those shows, the 150-seat studio can only accommodate so many, so the network holds a twice-a-year lottery. Sign up online at www.foodtv.com or send your postcards to:

Emeril Live Ticket Lottery
P.O. Box 52151
Knoxville, TN 37950

There's no guarantee of food (counter tasters are randomly chosen), but one can always hope.

THE JANE PAULEY SHOW
NBC Studios
**30 Rockefeller Plaza (6th Ave. bet. 49th &
50th Sts.) Midtown 212.664.3056**

A week after she retired from *Dateline*, Jane Pauley decided she'd had enough of the ambling life and took up residence in Rosie O'Donnell's former studio. This new talk show, to be slated into the tricky time slot head to head with Oprah, is scheduled to start in fall of 2004. If you want to be in on the action, call the studio to find out about audience options.

LAST CALL WITH CARSON DALY
NBC Studios
**30 Rockefeller Plaza (6th Ave. bet. 49th &
50th Sts.) Midtown 888.4LC.TIXX**

MTV is across the street from NBC. After his day job Mondays to Wednesdays, Carson runs over to tape another show. In its second season, *Last Call* comes on right after Conan O'Brien (at 1:30am, the VJ has bragging rights for the #1 show in its time slot). The good news: Not a lot of people know about *Last Call*, so the waiting time is typically no more than a week. Carson usually has a good lineup of celebrities (Angelina Jolie was on a recent show) with an emphasis on musical guests (both up-and-coming rock bands and established musicians). Note: If you get in, the network wants you to dress like you're going to a club, minus the white, beige, or light blue clothing, and elaborate patterns and logos.

LATE NIGHT WITH CONAN O'BRIEN
NBC Studios
30 Rockefeller Plaza (6th Ave. bet. 49th & 50th Sts.) Midtown 212.664.3056

After more than 10 years, Conan hasn't lost his standing as the original Irish jackass. When it's not on hiatus, the show tapes late Tuesday-Friday afternoons for an hour. You'll see the writers and producers in action, getting the cue cards ready between takes. Call six months in advance to reserve up to four tickets, or make it easy on yourself and get stand-by tickets the same day of the show, at 30 Rockefeller Plaza at 9am.

THE LATE SHOW WITH DAVID LETTERMAN
CBS Studios
51 W. 52nd St. (5th & 6th Aves.) Midtown 212.975.4321

Getting to see Dave and *The Late Show* against the not-so-live backdrop of the city is one of the most exciting things you can do in New York. It takes patience, though: Tapings—which occur late afternoons Monday through Thursday—are often booked nine months to a year in advance. There are a few ways to get the tickets. You can request them by sending a postcard with your name, address, and daytime and evening phone numbers to:

Late Show Tickets
The Ed Sullivan Theater
1697 Broadway
New York, NY 10019

Of course, this is deceptively straightforward. There's also an Internet ticket contest, which seems redundant, given that (a) you have to jump through a few hoops to win, and (b) tickets are free on request anyhow. To score one, send a letter to the same address as above, but address it to THE LATE SHOW INTERNET TICKET CONTEST (in all caps), 8th Floor. In addition to basic contact details, include:

1) Why you want tickets (duh),
2) The person you'd bring and why, and
3) Your favorite show moments

But the best way is to call the standby phone number (212.247.6497) at 11am. The phones are manned by people until the tickets are gone, then you get a recording. If you get through, you get assigned a standby number, but it doesn't guarantee you a seat—you still have to show up in the standby stampede and hope your number comes up. You're most apt to luck out on a Thursday, when they tape double shows—one for that night, and one for Friday.

LIVE WITH REGIS AND KELLY
7 Lincoln Sq. (W. 67th St. & Columbus Ave.)
Upper West Side

So if you're dying to see Regis and Kelly in the flesh, and you can't wait a year to do it, the good news is there's a standby line (a cure I can't help you with). You do need to get to the studio at 7am for a standby number, and even then, there is no guarantee. (If you really have nothing better to do with your morning, go for it.) The long way: Send a postcard with your name, address, preferred dates, phone number, and number of tickets (up to four) to: Live Tickets, Ansonia Station, P.O. Box 230777, New York, NY 10023-0777.

SATURDAY NIGHT LIVE
NBC Studios
30 Rockefeller Plaza (6th Ave. bet. 49th & 50th Sts.) Midtown 212.664.3056

For one of the longest-standing, most popular, and wholly live comedy acts in all of television history, it makes sense that this is the hardest ticket to get in show business. Call to enter your name in the computer lottery, which is held in the month of August for the whole of the October to May season. "Winners" are notified two weeks in advance of the show. (Can't make it? Your luck automatically goes to some fortunate standby candidate.) There's no option: If you're in, you're slotted for either the two-hour dress rehearsal or the 90-minute taping at 11:30pm—truly live, with no technical delays. Either option's a good one: The perennially excellent improvs are often funnier than the original sketches. And on the flip side, you get to see the occasional screw-up.

THE VIEW
ABC Studios
320 W. 66th St. (@ West End Ave.)
Upper West Side

Tickets are given out on a first-come, first-served policy, with a current waiting time of nine months. You're notified three weeks prior to the show date. Fill out the short and simple online form (http://abc.go.com/theview/tickets/tickets.html), or send a postcard with relevant information to:

Tickets for The View
320 W. 66th St.
New York, NY 10023

There's also a standby line. Be at the studio before 9:30am.

2 GOOD LOOKIN' *cheap*

There really are few excuses for not looking good. Money is certainly not one of them. In this big city, you have all kinds of primpers and preeners at your disposal, and not all of them charge exorbitant sums for doing what nature didn't. We tell you how to build the bionic you, whether you're outdoors or in.

For staying in shape there is the obvious: miles of traverses for jogging, rollerblading, and cycling, and reasonably priced gyms and exercise studios (yoga, boxing, self-defense, Pilates) on every block. Meanwhile, the city, which has a vested interest in keeping you fit (less money spent on health-

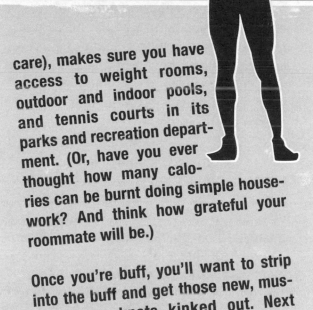

care), makes sure you have access to weight rooms, outdoor and indoor pools, and tennis courts in its parks and recreation department. (Or, have you ever thought how many calories can be burnt doing simple housework? And think how grateful your roommate will be.)

Once you're buff, you'll want to strip into the buff and get those new, muscle-strewn knots kinked out. Next come new duds, and then an all-out attack on your skin: dead or alive.

If you need a little structure in your workout, there are plenty of ways to get it without blowing your monthly budget. Gyms are great all-around options offering weather-proof workouts and the one-stop-shopping of weight and cardio facilities, yoga, boxing, and other classes, and maybe a pool. But if you like the idea of specializing in something like yoga, consider paying a periodic fee to make unlimited trips to a studio.

NOTE: When buying any membership, remember that there is never a bad time for negotiation, and that the worst thing you can be told is no. Gyms want your money: Think outside the box, and get yourself a discount on new workout clothes, a personalized locker, or one or two free personal training sessions.

BALLY TOTAL FITNESS
Various locations in NYC, including:

144–146 E. 86th St. (Lexington & 3rd Aves.)
Upper East Side 212.722.7371

45 E. 55th St. (@ Madison Ave.)
Midtown 212.688.6630

350 W. 50th St. (8th & 9th Aves.)
Midtown 212.265.9400

335 Madison Ave. (@ 43rd St.)
Midtown 212.983.5320

139 W. 32nd St. (6th & 7th Aves.)
Midtown 212.465.1750

641 6th Ave. (19th & 20th Sts.)
Chelsea 212.645.4565

75-28 Queens Blvd. (74th & 76th Sts.)
Elmhurst 718.898.5533

Sure, Bally's has more passé than it does caché, but the fact that you even care illustrates a loopy concept in gym fitness—that the place where you sweat has to achieve any image at all. If that doesn't convince you, try this: If all you want is a traditional workout (read: weight training and/or cardiovascular fitness), with little in the way of hoops and frills (a cutting-edge trainer, frilly yoga, the latest fad workout), then the extra money you spend going to a gym with caché joins the sweaty vapor that surrounds that rush-hour dash to the treadmills.

By paying $40-$60 or less a month (compared to $80+ at Equinox, Reebok, Crunch, or other more luxurious clubs), you'll have more left over to put into some new clothes after you're done sculpting your hot new figure. Here's how you do it. First, pick your gym, and set yourself up with a free two-week guest pass, which you can print out from the website (www.ballyfitness.com). You're going to have to meet a salesperson, take a tour, and sit through a sales pitch, but don't worry: You've already made your mind up to join. Next, check out the gym's frequent specials, such as a three-day workout (you pick the days) for $19 a month, a $5 startup amount, or $50 off for new college graduates. That's it. Come see us again when you've gotten rid of that unsightly fat around your knees.

Be Yoga

138 5th Ave., 4th Fl. (@ 19th St.)
Flatiron 212.647.9642

1319 3rd Ave., 2nd Fl. (75th & 76th Sts.)
Upper East Side 212.650.9642

160 E. 56th St., 12th Fl. (3rd & Lexington Aves.)
Midtown 212.935.9642

If you like your yoga to strike a balance between athletic and nurturing, then Be Yoga—founded by Alan Finger as the former Yoga Zone—may have your mudras. The studio has a recession-buster rate: $40 for two weeks of unlimited classes at any of the three locations. If you're a daily yogi, that's $240 off of the à la carte rate of $20 per class. (After that, staying loyal to Finger's original brand of ISHTA yoga gets a lot pricier, even with the $225 monthly unlimited rate.)

Dolphin Fitness Clubs

Various locations in NYC, including:

209 W. 125th St. (@ 7th Ave.)
Harlem 212.864.0200

330 E. 59th St. (1st & 2nd Aves.)
Midtown 212.486.6966

50 E. 42nd St. (Park & Madison Aves.)
Midtown 212.286.0999

242 E. 14th St. (2nd & 3rd Aves.)
East Village 212.614.0390

94 E. 4th St. (1st & 2nd Aves.)
East Village 212.387.9500

155 E. 3rd St. (@ Ave. A)

East Village 212.533.0090

18 Ave. B (2nd & 3rd Sts.)
East Village 212.777.1001

90 John St. (@ Gold St.)
Financial District 212.732.4445

www.dolphinfitnessclubs.com

Dolphin's carving a nifty niche for itself: 25 clean, non-frilly locations in the tri-state area. True, there's an imbalance of gyms in the East Village and Staten Island, but be patient: This gym is growing fast. What you get is bare-bones basics: new or nearly new equipment, group classes in aerobics, yoga, weight-sculpting, Pilates, and boxing, and guest privileges (although you can't bring the same person more than once, and your guest has to listen to the sales spiel). Before you join, take advantage of the week-long trial period on offer. Then either look out for the cheap yearly special ($350-$400), or sign up online for a one- to three-month membership, at $30-$40 a month (for which you get two little bonuses: a free top-to-toe medical exam and three $50 certificates you can give to your friends).

HIMALAYAN INSTITUTE NEW YORK
78 5th Ave. (@ 13th St.)
Greenwich Village 212.243.5995

With its free meditation classes on Thursday nights, free sat-sang, and free introduction to yoga, this is a great place for an incoming student to get started. But as an intermediate, if you have a flexible schedule and are happy giving up class frequency for a more personal approach, then this Manhattan branch of the global nonprofit institute could easily be the best—never mind most economical—yoga center for you. Sixty- or 90-minute classes of varying levels happen at least four times a week, and cost from $10-$15 a session.

JEWISH COMMUNITY CENTER
The Samuel Priest Rose Building
334 Amsterdam Ave. (@ W. 76th St.)
Upper West Side
646.505.4444 (switchboard) or
646.505.5700 (membership)

There's nothing quite like the music of an indoor lap pool: Out of the water, sounds make great flying curves through the air; plunge your head in, and become ensconced in silence. If you're a swimmer, you can't let this deal pass you by. The JCC has a clean 25-meter lap pool heated to 82 degrees. You get a locker and clean towels. And membership for the pool is only $745 for the year, and half of $935 if you join with a family member (generally not a roommate, but co-habiting couples of any gender meet the criteria). (Access to the expanded portion of the fitness center—with state-of-the-art equipment—is much, much more.) Go in for one of the scheduled tours, and ask for a free day pass.

JIVAMUKTI YOGA CENTER
404 Lafayette St., 3rd Fl. (E. 4th St & Astor Pl.)
East Village 212.353.0214

853 Lexington Ave. (@ E. 64th St.)
Upper East Side 212.396.4200

If your chakras are out of whack, Jivamukti can whack 'em back. The top-notch center is surely one of the most expensive yoga centers in the city; not that the celebrity-strewn clientele—Madonna, Gwyneth—has any difficulty shelling out the $19 for each class, and then some for the designer yoga mat. Why is it in this book? First, both uptown and downtown locations give all new students one free introductory class—call ahead for the day and time. But even better, every Monday night at 8pm, Jivamukti hosts Kirtan. (To those uninitiated, that's an extended, musical version of the call and response chanting that happens at the start of your yoga class.) The musicians are top-notch, coddling you into the rhythm with smooth voices and exotic instruments before you can uncross your legs, clasp your fingers, and utter "Namastay." For this modern-day version of 1960s mood-alteration music, donations are appreciated.

McBURNEY YMCA
125 W. 14th St. (6th & 7th Aves.)
West Village 212.741.9210

At $76/month ($57 for students), membership at this Y isn't rock-bottom cheap, but the 16-class series is. For $170, any non-member can sign up for bodysculpting, kickboxing, tai chi, ballet, yoga, and Pilates—the only restriction is that all 16 classes have to be taken within an eight-week period. Also, look into the Y's $12 classes in topics from art to job searches to comedy.

NEW YORK SPORTS CLUB

Various locations in NYC, including:
34 W. 14th St. (5th & 6th Aves.)
Greenwich Village 212.337.9900

113 E. 23rd St. (@ Park Ave. South)
Gramercy 212.982.4400

575 Lexington Ave. (@ 51st St.)
Midtown 212.317.9400

248 W. 80th St. (@ Broadway)
Upper West Side 212.873.1500

Visibility and concentration are priceless business concepts, and NYSC has got both going for it. With 36 clubs in Manhattan and slightly fewer in the outer boroughs and New Jersey, the red and white logo is everywhere to remind you not to laze off. Workout-wise, not much gets left to the imagination; for starters, the gyms' offerings include more than 115 class types. There are nice touches: If you're not familiar with strength-training equipment, the club offers a program called Xpress Line, a 22-minute trainer-supervised weight circuit, staffed at various times throughout the day. After your free week trial, it costs $85 or so to join (to beat that rate, look for deals online (www.mysportsclubs.com) or in ads towards the end of the month). Once you're in, there are a few tiers of membership: Passport memberships—great for travelers—allow entry to the corporate owner's clubs in D.C., Philly, and Boston (average monthly passport fee is $90); gold memberships ($65) make one club your primary location, with rights to work out at other clubs during defined, off-peak hours. Other than the convenient locations, 95% of the customer base keeps it non-committal: month-to-month memberships—it's even possible to freeze your membership if you go away.

SIVANANDA YOGA VEDANTA CENTER
243 W. 24th St. (7th & 8th Aves.)
Chelsea 212.255.4560

This tiny, non-frenetic yoga center is truly yoga for the people. Your first class is always free. More poignantly, Sivananda hosts free monthly open houses to introduce newbies to yoga—as a practice but also as a lifestyle. The all-day Saturday walk-in program begins with a lecture, then proceeds to one-hour yoga classes both before and after the vegetarian lunch. If you get hooked, joining would be one of the best things you can do for your body and your wallet: This studio is one of the best values in town. Individual classes (60 and 90 minutes) start at $12 ($10 for students), versus the $16+ charged at fancy, big-name studios. It gets even better, at $35 for a week of unlimited classes, $75 for a month, $175 for three months, and $500 for a year. It's a wonder the tiny practice room doesn't get mobbed

FITNESS IN A BOOK

If you think coupons have no place in the big city, think again. The Fitness Access PassBook is brought to you in part by our federal government, mortified by our national weight problem. The PassBook gives you 400 coupons to use at gyms all over the city—perfect if you're shopping for a new gym. You have a year to use the coupons. Some highlights: a week at Bikram Yoga (the sweaty kind), a whopping three weeks at Dolphin Fitness Clubs, 10 personal training sessions at various gyms, Pilates, martial arts, swimming, fencing...you get the idea. Commune and save even more: buy three and get one free. The only drawback is the scrambling; on the bright side, haven't you just always wanted to check out Lenox Hill? There is also a similar PassBook for yogis containing 250 passes. Uncle Sam wants you...to keep your new body: When you join any gym on the list, you get your $65 back.

FITNESS PASSBOOK
American Health and Fitness Alliance
212.808.0765
www.health-fitness.org

Some of us forget that staying in shape doesn't always require running on a treadmill à la hamsters. Workouts don't have to be so, well, workout-intense all the time; it's nice if you can play while upping your fitness quotient, and enjoy the company.

A note on pick-up games: If you've got a favorite sport, then there's no reason you can't dive right in. All the major parks and sport courts in the city have pick-up everything from basketball to touch football to Frisbee, and they're nothing to turn your nose up at. The guys and girls who participate are good, and they're competitive.

CENTRAL PARK SKATE PATROL
72nd St. (Central Park)

For new in-liners looking for a free lesson in how to stop, the Central Park Skate Patrol hosts a stopping clinic at both the E. and W. 72nd Street entrances to the park. The lessons are held on weekend afternoons during prime skating season, mid-April to mid-October.

CITY CLIMBERS CLUB
59th Street Gym
533 W. 59th St. (10th & 11th Aves.)
Midtown 212.974.2250

Rock climbers in the know still rave about the city's first indoor rock climbing gym. With 11 belay stations, it's hardly the biggest around, but the dozens of do-it-yourself routes and realistic bouldering obstacles and mock cave have wide appeal. Joining the gym costs $200 a year, and the one-time $12 use fee is far lower than the $50 charged at Chelsea Piers. Best of all, the gym is a great place to hand-select companions for a trip to rock climbers' mecca: the Gunks in New Paltz. Note: The indoor wall at the Central Park Conservancy could—with its $5 use fee—give CCC a run for its money. The bad news? The 12-foot structure is open on a limited schedule.

DOWNTOWN BOATHOUSE (KAYAKING)
Pier 26 (Chambers & Canal Sts.) &
Pier 66A (@ 27th St.)
Hudson River Park 646.613.0375

Don't worry, no one's going to make you drop into an Eskimo roll. In fact, there's nothing here even vaguely resembling Eskimos or rolls: The boathouse is only open in warm weather (late spring to mid-fall), when it's possible to do laps on the Hudson. The program takes you through baby steps: If you've never kayaked before, start with an introductory class (call ahead—not all classes are for beginners). Next, drop by for a paddle, lifejacket, and kayak to take on a 20-minute jaunt into a fenced enclosure. (The self-bailing, one-to-two-person kayaks might keep your bum soaked until the holes in the bottom of the boat have had a chance to drain.) After you've done this a couple of times, you can sign up for one of the guided weekend trips—three hours to go five miles. Demand is typically high—if there are more people than boats, they'll stage a lottery.

E. 6TH STREET TRACK
E. 6th St. (on the East River)
Lower East Side

And if you're a runner with a simple hankering for the same kind of outdoor track you ran on in high school, then the E. 6th Street track is all you need. Four laps equal one mile on this soft, rubberized running surface. Distances of 100, 110, and 200 meters are also clearly marked. The view of the East River, Brooklyn, and Queens is a bonus.

FIVE BOROUGH BICYCLE CLUB
New York International Youth Hostel
891 Amsterdam Ave., # 101 (102nd & 103rd Sts.) Upper West Side 212.932.2300 ext. 115

For $20—half the membership fee of other clubs—you can buy yourself an entirely new lifestyle: a fit one, with fun activities and over 1,000 insta-companions, all of whom are fit like you. All you need is a bike and the membership fee ($25 for two in the same household). Of course, the Five Borough Bicycle Club's central activity is Bike New York, the five-borough tour that happens in early May—and draws upwards of 30,000 attendees (nothing like the deafening roar of Queensites greeting you  beyond the Queensboro Bridge). Going further? Graduate to the 5BBC's Montauk Century Tour, which is a 140-mile jaunt straight out to the tip of Long Island.

There's plenty of other stuff happening throughout the year. Many of the 40-50-mile weekend day rides are free. There's no chance of getting bored, since ride themes are downright fascinating. Take, for example, the "War of the Worlds" ride, in which cyclists visit the New Jersey site where the Martians supposedly landed during Orson Welles' panic-inducing Mercury Theater broadcast. And the club offers useful courses for a small fee, such as how to fix a flat tire, and how to keep your training active through wintertime. And yes, the cyclist club does travel through all five boroughs, with a special emphasis on the greenways—new and old—of Manhattan and Staten Island. Note: If you join the club, your $50 entrance fee to Bike New York is waived.

NEW YORK CITY PARKS AND RECREATION
Various locations throughout NYC
212.360.3300

Because we're all too busy donating thousands of dollars to gyms that don't need money, very few people know how you can work out for absolutely free. The city has over 1,700 parks and facilities comprising 28,000 acres. That includes 53 free outdoor pools, 10 free indoor pools, 550 tennis courts, 614 playing fields, 14 miles of beaches, 991 playgrounds, 13 golf courses, and 4 zoos. The options aren't limited to the facilities; lessons are free, too. Check out endless options: golf instruction, in-line skating, basketball, and soccer clinics.

NIKETOWN RUNNING CLUB
6 E. 57th St. (Madison & 5th Aves.)
Midtown 212.891.6453

You might think you train better on your own, but there's nothing like a fast group and a top running coach to push you beyond your limits. The weekly runs in Central Park attract beginners, too, but they'll be people to make sure you get the most of the money you didn't pay to join. And afterwards, you can enjoy munchies to put some needed weight back on that frame of yours—'cuz I don't know, you're starting to look a little gaunt.

Outdoor Pools in Manhattan

Call ahead to find out the rules at specific pools. At Carmine, for example, dyed clothing is forbidden lest you taint the waters, so bring a white T-shirt and white shorts.

Asser Levy (Asser Levy Pl. & E. 23rd St.)
Gramercy 212.447.2020

Carmine (Clarkson St. & 7th Ave. South)
West Village 212.242.5228

Dry Dock (E. 10th St. @ Aves. C & D)
East Village 212.677.4481

Hamilton Fish (Pitt & Houston Sts.)
Lower East Side 212.387.7687

Highbridge (Amsterdam Ave. & 173rd St.)
Harlem 212.927.2400

Jackie Robinson (Bradhurst Ave. & 146th St.)
Harlem 212.234.9607

John Jay (York Ave. @ 77th St.)
Upper East Side 212.794.6566

Lasker (W. 110th St. & Lenox Ave.)
Harlem 212.534.7639

Marcus Garvey (124th St. & 5th Ave.)
Harlem 212.410.2818

Sheltering Arms
(W. 129th St. & Amsterdam Ave.)
Harlem 212.662.6191

Thomas Jefferson (112th St. & 1st Ave.)
Harlem 212.860.1372

Wagner (E. 124th St. bet. 1st & 2nd Aves.)
Harlem 212.534.4238

RANDALL'S ISLAND
Tennis Center 212.534.4845
Tennis Reservations 212.860.2863
Golf Center and Batting Cages 212.427.5689

The large green land mass tucked handily beneath the Triborough Bridge offers golf, tennis, and batting practice for less money and less hassle than their Manhattan counterparts.

The distance of the nonresidential island from Manhattan can be measured in yards. In MTA lingo, what it means is a short ride from Manhattan on the Lexington Avenue line, then a transfer to the M35 bus. Once there, check out the island's Tennis Center: 11 outdoor courts, four of which get converted into indoor courts during cold weather. Playing on Randall's outdoor courts requires the same $100 permit that you get from Parks & Recreation (covers you from April to November; 212.360.8131). But at most, you'll wait about 20 minutes until a court frees up. In the winter, indoor courts are the cheapest in the city—at $38-$58 per hour.

Next door, there is a nine-station batting cage for grand-slamming your frustrations away, which costs $2 for 15 pitches. And if swinging a wooden stick doesn't do the trick, try iron: The nearby Golf Center, a bargain at only $12 for 119 balls, has an 80-station driving range. (Tuesday through Friday during the off-peak hours of 6am-11pm, your bucket contains 170 balls for the same price.) Afterwards, $6 gives you a little putt-putt action in the two 18-hole miniature golf courses, including equipment. Nope, the courses don't contain any trickster gadgets to ruin the chances of your hole in one. But they do offer some really nice, manicured lawns, with flowers in seasonal bloom.

BONUS: Randall's also houses soccer fields—call for details.

CHEAP SKATE

Sure, you say. Ice skating and Christmas go hand in hand. But where do the would-be Kristy Yamaguchis go at the other times of the year? Easy: ice rinks that slash prices after the sport's oh-so-brief high season. In the case of Chelsea Piers, we're talking way after: The indoor ice rink—open year-round, offers free summer skating on Saturdays between 2pm–4pm. From December until March, Central Park's Wollman Rink often decides to cut the admission in half for its "free skate" on select weekday evenings (although call first to confirm). Meanwhile, Lasker Rink is Wollman's uptown alternative, and skating there is only $4.50 even in prime skate season. Even higher up, you can practice your hockey stops along the West Side Highway, in the canopied hockey rink that charges the same price for public weekend skates. Or leave the borough entirely and go to Wollman Rink's better half: Kate Wollman Rink, in Prospect Park. Rentals are extra.

CHELSEA PIERS
Pier 61 (23rd St. & Hudson River)
Chelsea 212.336.6100

KATE WOLLMAN RINK
(East Dr. & Lincoln Rd.)
Prospect Park 718.287.6431

LASKER RINK
Mid-Park (108th & 109th Sts.)
Central Park 212.534.7639

RIVERBANK STATE PARK
Riverside Dr. (@ 145th St.)
Upper West Side 212.694.3642

WOLLMAN RINK
W. 59th St. entrance (walk 3 minutes north)
Central Park 212.439.6900

After all that physical exertion, you're going to need restoration for your sore muscles. For a small sacrifice (be it to privacy, ambiance, or the chi-chi factor that the fancy spas can eject right out of their blowholes), all of the following venues can do it for less.

RUSSIAN TURKISH BATHS
268 E. 10th St. (1st Ave. & Ave. A)
East Village 212.473.8806

If you think of this as a bath, it's a plain rip-off. It costs $22 a trip to take a hot water dip, which you can get for free at home—so long as you have a tub. But then you'd be missing the point. The hot bath at this newly renovated East Village standby is far hotter, the cold plunge more bracing, and the company more fascinating than any soak you can conjure in your homey porcelain number. $22 (or less if you get a 10- or 15-use pass) entitles you to use of the hot bath, steam room, redwood sauna, ice-cold pool, sundeck, locks, lockers, robes, towels, shorts, and slippers. Walk-in treatments are also available. Get yourself rubbed with salt ($34) or oil (about $1/minute), slathered with mud ($38), or beaten with an oak branch (it's plaetza, not S&M). Ahhh…

SOL SPA
4 W. 33rd St. (5th & 6th Aves.)
Midtown 212.564.2100

For $120 this modern spa can give you a treatment that easily costs $300 outside of this Korean neighborhood. The first step involves two saunas—one dry and one steam (the longer you can stand it the better, as it will make the rest of the treatment more effective). You'll lie on a not-so-private table. One woman will give you a mini-facial with mashed, fresh cucumbers, while another scrubs your entire body like a pig in pasture. You're led into a private massage room, where you receive a 50-minute deep tissue massage with a moist, seaweed emollient. Then it's back to the wet room, where you're cleansed from the scalp on down like they really mean it. The whole thing takes about two hours. You will leave with baby soft skin.

NOTE: You must be comfortable being nude. If privacy's important, you might want to go during a quiet weekday afternoon.

SWEDISH INSTITUTE
226 W. 26th St. (7th & 8th Aves.)
Chelsea 212.924.5900

The Swedish Institute has been teaching the arts of herbalism, acupuncture, and massage to nurturing souls since 1969. If you don't mind volunteering your body, then a dirt cheap New Yorker has three possible ways to benefit. The first is a six-week stress-reduction series of relaxation massage, which costs $125 for weekly six-minute sessions (weekends only). Double your pain claim, double your pleasure—the therapeutic 12-week sessions, which combine Eastern and Western methods, cost $225 (weekends only). Or you can just opt for the pain, and sign up for acupuncture to improve your respiratory ailments, PMS, digestive disturbances, and other health issues, even infertility. For $300, including the initial consultation, you can receive 13 one-hour acupuncture sessions.

Of course there's a catch. Patience and perseverance, dahling: The massage clinic gets 3,000-4,000 applications a year.

TUI-NA
222 Lafayette St. (Spring & Kenmare Sts.)
NoLita 212.941.6038

This is one of the better Chinatown massage parlors, without actually being in Chinatown. As with other Chinese-run spots, you buy your massage in 10-minute increments; the more time you clock, the more the price drops from the roughly $1/minute starting rate. You may as well go for the full $40 hour, since—unlike with nearby massage places—you're going to get undressed, yes, in a big communal, coed room. For some, this will stir excitement in the loins—if you're not among those numbers, though, don't worry: Your neighbors are too ensconced in the microscopic precision of the acupressure to be gazing at you in all your naked glory.

YI PAK SPA
10 W. 32nd St. 2nd Fl. (5th Ave. & Broadway)
Midtown 212.594.1025

The $100 package just went up to $120, but it's still a good deal. Plan to spend a little over two hours getting pampered. You're shown into a locker room where you disrobe. You can take your time at the next step, dry and steam saunas for opening your pores while you linger in the heat. You're shown into a big wet room where you lie on one among several tables and get scrubbed everywhere (between the toes) until your skin turns rosy pink. Then comes the water—lots of it—so much the treatment staff dons underwear. An hour-long baby oil massage follows, followed by a fresh facial, shampoo, and scalp massage.

NOTE: You must be comfortable being nude. If privacy's important, you might want to take a few hours off on a weekday afternoon.

There's always an excuse to beautify your-self, whether you have a new job, a date, or just a stupid pimple. Well, shaping and adorning your dead skin cells—which is what it always comes down to, when you think about it—really doesn't have to be expensive. With NYC's plethora of beauty schools, reasonably priced nail salons, and off-the-beaten-track treatments, reaping the beauty inside will take a little explo-ration, but not a lot of money or hassle.

ATLAS BARBER SCHOOL
32 3rd Ave. (9th & 10th Sts.)
East Village 212.475.1360

80 E. 10th St. (3rd & 4th Aves.)
East Village 212.475.5699

In most cases, beauty salons are for making pretty, whereas barber schools are for making presentable. But presentable to one may be luminous to another; beauty after all is in the eye of your date. And both—no matter what you manly men might claim—are for pampering. This is a unisex barber shop, which isn't to say that they make all customers look androgynous. However, I wouldn't advise the girls to go there, unless all you need is the most basic trim (nothing's styled, and the 60-some students are here to learn men's barbering). Cuts are $4 on 10th Street, $5 at 3rd Avenue (the difference is based on the number of chairs at each location), shaves $2, and the 15-20 min. cold cream facial massages $5. See what I mean about pampering?

AVEDA INSTITUTE
233 Spring St. (6th Ave. & Varick St.)
SoHo 212.807.1492 ext. 2

The on-premises student institute at this calming, nurturing salon offers a wide range of services at drastically reduced rates. The students are supervised, although their level and the level of supervision are the luck of the draw (the salon doesn't take requests for advanced students). Need your locks blessed? Haircuts and heat styling are only $15, and—although satisfaction is not guaranteed and your cut might take as long as two hours—you're totally not subject to some instructor's random curriculum (i.e., finding out you've scheduled your appointment on crewcut day). Similarly, updos, perms, and highlights start at $20. As for those blackheads, the aesthetician students need models, too: A 45 minutc trcatment will run you $45, and a 90-minute only $55. Waxing is not as good of a deal: Baring your upper lip or shaping your brows is $10, and a full leg will run you $35. Classes have to be in session, and there is an estimated four-week waiting period for a Saturday appointment.

BERGDORF GOODMAN—BEAUTY LEVEL
754 5th Ave. (@ 58th St.)
Midtown 1.800.558.1855

Blinding white light, smiling faces, freebies galore, and no easily discernible way out. No, you're not in heaven, although for the beauty addict, the heavenly conceived Beauty Level at Bergdorf Goodman comes close. Two or three times a year (usually during the change of seasons and holidays), Bergdorf sends out mailers for a beauty day. The mailer is worth $25 of free cosmetics with a $50 purchase—do the math, and you're pretty well off. At all other times, come into this beauty emporium to try, buy, and be treated like a princess (Bergdorf's has a generous, no-questions-asked return policy).

BUMBLE & BUMBLE
415 W. 14th St. (9th & Washington Sts.)
West Village 917.606.5000

Model calls are held Mondays from 5:30pm-6:30pm. It's hardly a cattle call; you see a stylist and they give you a little once-over before you can make an appointment. You're donating your hair and not just your cuddly, adorable self, but that doesn't mean you can't get the cut of your dreams. Best of all, the people trying hard to make you look good are working stylists from around the country who come to NYC to brush up on their skills—not students. And it's not just a one shot deal: Once you're enrolled, it's more or less free haircuts for life.

DYANNA
40 E. 21st St. (Park Ave. South & Broadway)
Flatiron 212.995.2355

150 E. 39th St. (Lexington & 3rd Aves.)
Murray Hill 212.213.0011

"This is bikini city," says owner Mona Winograd, saying goodbye to another happy recipient of the fast and amazing $25 Brazilian. The salon, which originated in Murray Hill over twenty years ago, is one of a dying breed of shops where the proprietors know everyone by name. Although models and movie people have joined the mothers and grandmothers who bring in babies ("we've been known to change diapers," says Mona), the place gives off bushels of neighborhood aura, and the prices remain beyond reasonable. Waxing—quick and precise—ranges from $5-$40, a basic manicure is $11, and a pedicure $20. Keep your eyes—or legs—peeled for cold weather specials.

JENIETTE DAY SPA
58 E. 13th St. (University Pl. & Broadway)
Greenwich Village 212.529.1616

Owner Jeniette Melamed uses a few tricks from Iran. One of them is eyebrow threading—a more precise, albeit slower alternative to waxing, and she claims to have been the first to offer it to New Yorkers. But hair removal isn't all this full-service spa performs. Jeniette is on the below-average side of the pricing scale, a situation belied by the aesthetic touches that make this a lovelier-than-usual salon: Basic manicures run only $10. There are two ways to guarantee paying even less. Come on a Monday or Tuesday, and pay $50 (compared with $60) for a facial, and $27 (compared with $31) for a basic mani and pedi. Or try a package: Buy 10 manicures, five facials ($60 and up), or five one-hour massages ($75) and get one of the same for free.

KIEHL'S
109 3rd Ave. (13th & 14th Sts.)
East Village 212.677.3171

150 years ago there was a pharmacy on this spot. That pharmacy has grown up now, and it is a multinational conglomerate that sells darn-good all-natural products for hair and skin. But old-fashioned ways die hard, and the company—which doesn't believe in advertising—does believe in giving out samples, which makes this store a grab-bag of opportunity, from two- and three-use bubbles to miniature bottles. Everyone has a Kiehl's favorite, and I'll share mine: the pale, herbal shampoo.

THE CHINATOWN FACIAL

Downtown and uptown, New York City is filled with nicey-nice salons. These may look and smell good, but the gentle aestheticians that coddle you and dab ever so delicately at your pimples are way too tentative to make your skin feel like it's been through a workout. Those facials are over before you can muster the wherewithal to peep, "More pressure, please."

In Asian mega-communities like Chinatown, Koreatown, Flushing, and Sunset Park, not only will you pay about $30-40 for 90 minutes to two hours, but you get a workout—oh boy! The facialists—often immigrants who generally know at least as much English to ask questions like, "Combination skin?"—treat skin with the precision of laser technicians...and such vigor!

Expect the usual: cleansing, exfoliation, steam, ionization, de-blackheading, and mask (sometimes you'll get two either consecutively or simultaneously). Somewhere between two steps the facialist will apply liberal amounts of massage cream, and you will learn the true meaning of the ancient Chinese nickname "Thunder Fingers." The massage will typically go on for 20 or 30 minutes—take a chi-chi massage uptown and divide it in half. Afterwards, you can feel the blood flowing.

Yes, they're using moistened tissues instead of Egyptian cotton finger towels, and yes, that is Chinese pop music blaring over the loudspeakers. And yes, you get to share your room with a few others (but really, how much benefit can you get from utter privacy buried under a mound of blankets with a layer of clay over your eyes?). If you can get over these minor details, your skin and your wallet will thank you.

NOTE: You can also get a haircut for $10, but these are a little more hit or miss. You can get a decent cut, and as an added bonus, the shampoo person will often give you a little scalp massage before turning the clippers loose on you. But hey, don't come crying to us if you come out of the salon looking like a cat that got run over by a lawnmower.

JOEAN SKIN CARE
163 Hester St. (Elizabeth & Mott Sts.)
Chinatown 212.966.3668

KATRINA SKIN CARE INC
187 Centre St. (@ Hester St.)
Chinatown 212.966.9531

SAI KAY BEAUTY
163 Mott St. (Grand & Broome Sts.)
Chinatown 212.226.5302

MIDAS NAILS
203 W. 14th St., 2nd Fl. (@ 7th Ave.)
West Village 646.230.7259

Know this from the start: Whether they're busy or not, the Korean nail technicians are going to be done with your nails before you can say "cut cuticles." Having said that, no one's rushing you out of the roomy second-floor loft: You'll get the obligatory end-of-treatment neck rub and dry your perfect ten (or 20) at leisure. These days, the price of efficiency is pretty good: Come on a Monday, Tuesday, or Wednesday, and get a basic manicure and pedicure for $20. Manicures alone are always $7; pedicures $15 on those days and $17 towards or on the weekend.

SHISEIDO STUDIO
155 Spring St. (W. Broadway & Wooster St.)
SoHo 212.625.8820

You know the everything-for-a-dollar store? Well, this beats that: In the Shiseido Studio, everything is for free. Another way to say it is, nothing is for sale: This is one big teaser—one that will clean your face, do your makeup, and give you a few beauty-related tips for good measure. The studio is all about goodwill, as in "that mask is really good; will you be wanting to schedule a free mini-facial to learn how to use it?" Take 'em up on it; beyond mini-facials and the studio itself (a playland chock-full of product), there are personal makeovers, and classes on how to massage your face and neck, how to apply everyday makeup, and how to pamper and revive your senses. No, you won't go home with a bag of full-size products, unless you (a) steal it or (b) win the drawing held at the end of every class. And that would take getting a spot first—no small feat, considering how the word's gotten out. For classes, waiting time is a week or more; for personal treatments, we're talking five months.

Soon Beauty Lab
318 E. 11th St. (1st & 2nd Aves.)
East Village 212.260.4423

Soon-er is better than later, and when the timing is just so, you might find yourself a lucky, walk-in fool. When this streamlined salon trains new hair assistants (year-round), they'll be in need of models. You get a cut or color of your choice, a friendly beauty school grad to chat with for 90 minutes, and a supervising owner to make sure things don't go awry. The cut and style, ordinarily $45, is freer than body parts in a nudist beach. Colorings have fewer slots and book up faster—grab 'em (it's $10 for the chemicals fee).

You're buff, you're toned, you're beautiful...but you're still naked. This section ought to fix that.

CENTURY 21
22 Cortlandt St. (@ Broadway)
Financial District 212.227.9092

I know. The "best kept secret" has been out for ages. But we still have to mention it, if only to remind you of a way you can brighten any day—whether you need it or not. Everything in this emporium but cosmetics has been brought to a deep, deep discount. It reads like a regular department store: The basement floor carries home goods, 1st floor is men's and handbags, 2nd floor women's shoes and sportswear, 3rd floor designer collections, and so on. By designer I mean all the usual suspects: Ferre, D&G, Gaultier. I have spotted supple $400 Prada shoes for $90, and buttery, lace-up Plein Sud leather jackets, originally $2200, marked down to $600. Men can have a field day here as well; I found a Gucci jacket for $70 that would look very sharp on most guys. On the housewares end, I snagged a heavy duty rolling nylon suitcase by Samsonite, $40 from the original $100. Ladies: If they're not here to shop, leave the guys at home. They clutter the aisles like frightened bunny rabbits, making it difficult to use them as dressing rooms, or to sift through the racks with the maximum level of efficiency. Century 21's other locations are in Bay Ridge, Brooklyn, Westbury (upstate New York), Morristown, New Jersey, and an outlet for an outlet in Secaucus, New Jersey.

KNOCKOUT KNOCK-OFFS
ALONG CANAL STREET
IN CHINATOWN

This isn't a store, per se, but a street you might return from with a Louis Vuitton bag as real as a Pamela Anderson body part. A friend of mine recently bought just such a knock-off suitcase with a could-have-fooled-me label, but get this: Her $100 purchase is one well-made piece of happily ever after. Picture a durable leather exterior lined on the inside with a suppler grain perfectly matched. Bells and whistles—mesh pockets, handles, metal accents, the beige color, and logos—were all subdued, a coup d'etat for knock-off manufacturers for whom "over the top" used to be a point of pride. It's not that you couldn't tell whether it was real or fake (I couldn't): It happened to be a nicely stitched together piece of luggage for a very good price. Can you haggle with the shopkeeper? Sure! Will it get you anywhere? Depends on your resolve. How badly do you want that suitcase? How badly can you pretend?

THE ANNEX ANTIQUE FAIR AND FLEA MARKET

6th Ave. (24th & 26th Sts.)
Chelsea 212.243.5343
Saturdays & Sundays, sunrise to sunset

Up go the tarps, and in pour the well-heeled: every weekend, rain or shine. For urban pocket money, Sinbad's entire treasure chest is at your disposal, everything from vintage jeans to Himalayan jewelry, Irish linens to antique cameras, pocket watches and pens, and certainly furniture of all origins. A fox coat: $100. A pair of striking African nightstands: $50. And your fellow shoppers are no slummers: They're publicists and advertising types and buyers from Europe and Madison Avenue. Come back nearing closing time: at 5pm the dealer is either giving you a deal, or packing it in the back of his truck to haul back out to Connecticut or wherever. Don't miss concurrent antiquing at The Garage (112 W. 25th St.). Note for both: Fuel up on cash.

CHILL ON BROADWAY

427 Broadway (Canal & Howard Sts.)
Little Italy 212.343.2709

A chill is what you may well get from wearing the flirty clothes at this trendy, downtown store. $40 is the most you'll pay for anything in here, including an embroidered flare skirt lined with tulle ($25), shirred crop pants ($25), and leather high-heeled slip-ons ($35). The clothing might not last you 10 years, but these trends will change even faster than your feminine whims.

Find Outlet

229 Mott St. (@ Prince St.)
NoLita 212.226.5167

361 W. 17th St. (8th & 9th Aves.)
Chelsea 212.243.3177

Think outlet shopping for boutique designers, and you'll find it here. In other words, Find stocks never-worn fashions, some up to a few seasons old (but who's counting?) of the type you'd yank off the racks at Henri Bendel and Barneys—but for 50-80% less. The Chelsea branch is three times larger than the narrow NoLita shop, but at both places you're likely to find names like Jil Stuart, Vivienne Tam, Julia, and Mynt (a recent comb-through turned up a funky Japanese-style nubby wool cape by Viola, ordinarily $1200, for $225). The inventory is freshened up weekly, and if items don't sell within a couple of weeks, they withstand further markdowns. Twice a year the Chelsea store clears out its stock with huge sales that last five to six days, with prices as low as $10-$15.

H&M

125 W. 125th St. (Malcolm X Blvd. & Lenox Ave.) Harlem 212.665.8300

435 7th Ave. (@ 34th St.)
Midtown 212.643.6955

1328 Broadway (@ 34th St.)
Midtown 212.473.1165

640 5th Ave. (@ 51st St.)
Midtown 212.489.0390

558 Broadway (Prince & Spring Sts.)
SoHo 212.343.2722

**5100 King's Plaza Mall (Ave. U & E. 54th St.)
Mill Basin 718.252.5444**

Once upon a time, this was the little Swedish ready-to-wear chain that could. Now, it's a multinational fashion house that dresses the world in its private label…and passes the economies of scale down to you. From flare skirt to flared pantleg, the inexpensive clothing stylishly recaps all 50 years of its existence according to whatever's most inspired at the moment.

LUXURY BRAND OUTLET
**1222 2nd Ave. (@ 64th St.)
Upper East Side 212.734.2505**

The gang's all here: Prada, Manolo, Burberry, D&G. You could go mad with all the bargains from retail stores like Bergdorf Goodman: The company slashes high-end retail prices by up to 90%. Adorable California bathing suits, some with a sexy cutout hole, were $10 at season's end. Designer sunglasses and handbags are a standby: The rarely discounted Fendi baguette can be had for up to 45% off.

NEW AND ALMOST NEW
**166 Elizabeth St. (@ Kenmare St.)
NoLita 212.226.6677**

There are two kinds of consignment stores: the bulging or the slim. N&AN is undoubtedly the latter. After a decade in SoHo, the shop's new NoLita incarnation has a tidy, pared-down aesthetic, matched by its super-organized Hong Kong-born proprietor Maggie Poon. But don't think it's hit or miss: A recent after-hours stroll-through (Poon kindly unlocked the doors) yielded a pretty patchwork miniskirt by Tracey Feith ($40), navy Armani peacoat ($88), and Prada shoes galore (all about $150). I swooned over a funky Bottega bag made of pink pony fur and vinyl ($110) and a chocolate crocodile doctor's bag from the 1960s ($160). In fact, handbags and jewelry are particular strengths: supple $100 Ferragamos, beaded vintage numbers, rings, and other jewelry that manage to be both postmodern and vintage. Closed Mondays.

Nice Price SSS Sample Sale
261 W. 36th St., 2nd Fl. (7th & 8th Aves.)
Midtown 212.947.8745

If you hold it, they will come. A permanent sample sale, that is. And come they do—legions of women looking for true samples or overstock merchandise or other perfectly intact goodies from the likes of Nicole Farhi. Sometimes SSS hosts the sale, and sometimes, it merely rents the space out to a merchant who knows the word has gotten out.

Purdy Girl
220 Thompson St. (Bleecker & W. 3rd Sts.)
Greenwich Village 212.529.8385

The fashions here aren't just "purdy," they're downright pretty: floral skirts with lace in the trim, rabbit-lined sweaters with ribbing in the sleeves. A rolling rack that seems more like a fixture greets you outside the front door, displaying items for as low as $5 and $10 in a perma-sale. The trendy clothing comes in as swiftly as it moves out the door, and—at prices that represent a cut-rate off of the big department stores—it does move. Don't expect Barneys-like quality, but the clothing at least will last as long or longer as your taste.

GIRLS NIGHT OUT

Drinking and shopping so rarely combine—but they should. Three times a year, Shecky's dares you to put on your beer goggles and open your wallet. If this sounds ominous, know that you really can't go wrong. For $35, you're already ahead, with an instant goodie bag worth $100 (can't tell you what's in it, but Chanel and L'Oréal have both co-sponsored the event, if that gives you any clues). On top of that, you get access to 70-100 designers, five hours of open bar, and on-the-spot makeovers. You'll find lots of savvy cottage design that emphasizes the sexy (poured-on latex tops, challenge-me stilettos), the pretty (delicate neck beads, flirty dresses), and whimsical (fuzzy handbags, appliquéd knit thongs).

SHECKY'S
Various locations
212.242.2566
www.sheckys.com

496 Broadway (Spring & Broome Sts.)
SoHo 212.625.9552

This 2,000-square-foot emporium is all about jewelry. Amazingly, since a typical crystal necklace only takes up a few inches of display space. And yet the store is crammed with sparkling loveliness: intricate drop-crystal necklaces, chandelier earrings, inlaid silver barrettes (fake), and breath-takingly jeweled chignon sticks…even crystal-encrusted belts at what is undoubtedly the store's top price: $169 (most items hover around $10-$25). I can't say whether these Asian imports might last an eternity, but then again: How often are you going to wear that tiara, anyway?

RENEW YOUR SOLE

Take your favorite pair of boots: beautiful black leather ankle numbers with a side zip and a stylish two-inch heel. You put them on November 1st, and on your feet they stay until April 15th, come rain, snow, or sleet (you take them off to go to bed). They're now beaten-down and raggedy, with scuffed soles and a big embarrassing tear at the toe.

Well, it's time for a new pair of boots, right? Wrong. You take those babies and head for your local shoe repair shop. For $40 or less, these craftspeople will repair the hole, resole the base, buff and shine the entire thing, and generally return them to you in virgin condition. Well, almost virgin: They'll be as comfortable as you remember.

FACTORY CHEAP

Think of a trip to the outlet mall like grocery shopping in bulk: You don't need to go often. Two mega-centers come to mind.

WOODBURY COMMONS
PREMIUM OUTLETS
498 Red Apple Court
Central Valley, NY 845.928.4000

Nestled in a rural valley you'll be too busy to admire, Woodbury Commons is a dislocated Madison Avenue. You'd never have guessed the largely European name brands—Prada, Gucci, Frette, Miu Miu, even Chanel—had even bothered to secure American outlets. But there they sit—and seduce. Get a pair of supple Tod's loafers for half the full retail price, or an ornate La Perla bra for $25. As in any other mall, merchandise gets discounted even further at the end of a season—exactly the opposite of when you'd stock your produce drawers.

To get to Woodbury Commons, catch a ride on Shortline (800.631.8405). The air-conditioned coaches leave the Port Authority seven days a week nearly every hour starting from 7am to 7pm.

TANGER OUTLETS I, II, AND III
1770 W. Main St.
Riverhead, NY 631.369.2732

Promise me that at Christmastime, you'll avoid this place at all costs. It's not just crazy, it's downright life-threatening: The confluence of three adjacent shopping centers translates into a traffic maze being miserably untangled by direction monitors whose eyebrows have frozen into small white caterpillars.

At any other time, it's safe, and in fact eminently advisable to come shop. I have a routine, which involves snagging a cardboard box of juicy pears from Harry & David (discounted to about $1 per pear because of slight, non-detectable "blemishes") and a pair of new khakis from Banana Republic, then scouring the Nike store for great deals on running shoes and tights. You'll find some other of the usual outlet suspects: Jones New York, L'eggs, Maidenform, and Pepperidge Farm. Unlike at Woodbury Commons, there are few things you can actually splurge on in sensible Riverhead. Among them is furniture at ABC Home and Carpet (see Chapter 5).

Don't tell me you've never walked a mile in someone else's clothes. Well, don't you think it's time to fix that? Not only might you gain some empathy, but you also stand to get a significant discount off of name-brand clothes too valuable to throw away. Keep in mind that most consignment and donation shops require donors to wash the clothes beforehand.

Encore Designer Consignment
1132 Madison Ave. (84th & 85th Sts.)
Upper East Side 212.879.2850

No, you're not going to find any Juicy Couture peeking out amongst the Hermès and Dior. But you can't help loving this 50-year-old shop as you'd love a delicate little granny who wants to will you her precious pretties, to which she attaches substantial sentimental value if not a disproportionate price tag. Encore's buyers are super-selective, only accepting clothing and accessories that are a few years old and from the very top couturiers. Chanel suits can be found; also check out the great selection of handbags, including the ones in the glass cases.

Housing Works
157 E. 23rd St. (3rd & Lexington Aves.)
Gramercy 212.529.5955

306 Columbus Ave. (W. 74th & 75th Sts.)
Upper West Side 212.579.7566

202 E. 77th St. (2nd & 3rd Aves.)
Upper East Side 212.772.8461

143 W. 17th St. (6th & 7th Aves.)
Chelsea 212.366.0820

You can ascribe a lot of unsavory traits to New Yorkers, but there are two things you cannot fault us for: our generosity and our utter fashion savvy. When the two are combined, we are temporarily satiated, at least until it comes time to pick a take-out spot for dinner. Exonerate yourself at this all-donation joint. You can pick up some pretty unexpected things: a gently worn shearling coat, a spotless pair of men's calfskin boots, a set of Reidel crystal stemware. All proceeds go to the homeless, the recently homeless, or people with HIV/AIDS.

INA
101 Thompson St. (Prince & Spring Sts.)
SoHo 212.941.4757

The three women's—SoHo, NoLita, and the new UES— stores and the single men's store are tiny and selective, showcasing only what's trendy and funky, in season and madly coveted. You might find a teensy snakeskin Fendi bag for the unheard of $140, or approach a splurge with $345 for a buttery suede circle skirt—nowhere near the original $2,000.

MICHAEL'S
1041 Madison Ave. (79th & 80th Sts.)
Upper East Side 212.737.7273

This consignment store has the goods, and lots of them: two floors chock-full of pretty things for women, plus a bridal salon for the great day. Quantity is king. The store has more space and stocks itself fuller than nearby competitors. You might come across the occasional dowdy '80s suit, but for sheer selection, you can't go wrong. Prices get another 20% haircut every 30 days a garment sits in the store.

CULTURE *cheap*

It's time to revisit show business. Assuming for argument's sake that NYC is indeed the king of all things stage-worthy, you'd have to also agree that no other city competes with the strong cultural fixes that dot our urban landscape like so many pigeons pecking at scattered bread. This chapter—sweet on classical music, film, spoken word, education, and art—is intended to up the bread quotient...and hopefully inspire the culture vulture that lurks—yes, I said lurks—beneath. From free outdoor classical concerts to heavenly

choral performances at your neighborhood church, to low-budget film screenings and video rentals, to poetry readings, we've got your cultural bases covered.

This chapter will also show you how to enjoy the city's myriad fine museums on the cheap—or you can make your own art by taking one of the budget-friendly art classes we've listed here. Can't afford to bid on a Picasso? Art lovers can still take advantage of the city's auction houses. Just don't take anything home!

BRONX SYMPHONY ORCHESTRA
2141 Muliner Ave. (Pelham Pkwy. South & Lydig Ave.) Bronx 718.601.9151

It's all free, all the time. This talented orchestra has been putting on ticketless concerts for culture-hungry Bronxians and anyone else dedicated enough to venture on the dastardly subway ride. Check out www.bronxsymphony.org for concert schedules.

BROOKLYN BRIDGE PARK CONSERVANCY
DUMBO 718.802.0603

Keep your eyes peeled for a future event: Bargemusic's barge music concerts off of Brooklyn Bridge Park. These peaceful, chamber music concerts—performed on barges adjacent to Brooklyn Heights' River Café—ordinarily cost anywhere from $20-$40, but the Brooklyn Bridge Park Conservancy will be hosting free concerts in DUMBO starting in the summer of 2004.

BROOKLYN CONSERVATORY OF MUSIC
58 7th Ave. (@ Lincoln Pl.)
Park Slope 718.622.3300

42-76 Main St. (@ Northern Blvd.)
Flushing 718.461.8910

About five times a year, various faculty members of this fine conservatory put on recitals at each of the two locations. Watching a concert in the Brooklyn installment—a five-story Gothic mansion—is a total treat. Regular tickets are $10 and student prices $5. The conservatory also hosts "Jazz at the Conservatory" four times a year and "Music for Families" three times a year.

FRICK COLLECTION
1 E. 70th St. (Madison & 5th Aves.)
Upper East Side 212.288.0700

The lovely salon-like parlor converts to a performance room seating 175 lucky guests for periodic year-round concerts simulcast by WNYC. I say lucky because the private art collection has instituted the following insane process: To score your two free tickets, you have to time your mailed request, along with your self-addressed, stamped envelope, to arrive at the Frick Collection Concerts Department on precisely the third Monday prior to the concert (counting backwards). It's a bit of hoop jumping, but if you're a fan of chamber music, the ambiance will be worth it.

METROPOLITAN OPERA IN THE PARKS
Various Parks Citywide 212.362.6000

Notice the "s" after parks, since this free endeavor is by no means restricted to the Great Lawn of Central Park. No one can accuse the mighty Met of being non-democratic: The company travels to all five boroughs, and also New Haven and New Jersey. Thousands will show, so you need to get there early—and bring opera glasses. Performances are in June and August, giving the company July to re-coup and rehearse.

NEW YORK GRAND OPERA IN THE PARK
Naumburg Bandshell (off 72nd St. entrance)
Central Park 212.245.8837

The last time I went to a Grand Opera performance outdoors, some guy was selling T-shirts for the Met. When the sun goes down, the floodlight comes onto the elaborate performances of the Grand—typically familiar fare such as *La Boheme* and *Madame Butterfly*. There aren't any supertitles, so brush up on your Italian before you go...or get your hands on a lengthy, explanatory flyer.

NEW YORK PHILHARMONIC
Avery Fisher Hall
Lincoln Center (@ Broadway & W. 65th St.)
Upper West Side 212.875.5030

The New York Philharmonic and the word "bargain" don't usually go together, but there are two ways to see this venerable orchestra for unbelievable rates. If you've never been to a rehearsal, they are a fascinating lesson in leadership and artistic encouragement. The weekday open rehearsals begin at about 10am for two hours, and tickets cost $14. If you have a hankering to put on something fancier, then try the standby line on the day of a sold-out performance. If available, students and seniors pay $10 and non-students $27-$94, depending on the show. To find out if these are available, call the orchestra after 10am on the day of the concert.

SING IT TO THE RAFTERS

Nothing beats listening to music in the place God intended: a church. And I'm not just talking about the free choir perform-ances at Sunday mass. Churches often establish music programs to drum up more glory within their hallowed envi-rons; and, let's face it, to show off their gorgeous acoustics. Wouldn't you?

Starting downtown, Trinity Church is home in summer to a themed classical festival featuring acclaimed local performers. Don't be surprised to hear syncopated rhythms and/or a little dissonance: In 2003, Gershwin shared billing with Aaron Copland, and oh God it was glorious. Meanwhile, Chelsea's Church of the Holy Apostles gives its blessings to an ongoing handful of religious and non-religious choral, organ, and other instrumental con-certs. They're $10 ($20 for preferred seat-ing) to get in the door, and it's worth it just to get a look at the ornate organ that took four years to build.

In the fall, Saint Peter's Lutheran Church hosts a Basically Bach festival for $10-$15 (or $50 for all five concerts, if you're a real Bach fan). Then on Sunday afternoons at 5pm, Saint Peter's goes jazzy. The Christian pastoral ministry seeks "to create a relation-ship between God and the people who love jazz"; think of it as preachers with rhythm. The service is called Jazz Vespers, and brings in a broad range of jazz styles and musicians.

I'll never forget walking into Saint Thomas Church a little after Christmas one year, and hearing angels in the abbey. They were actually boys, and I'm sure out of their white gowns they're anything but heavenly, but it sure beat paying $50 the same year to hear a disappointingly faded recital by the Vienna Choir Boys at Carnegie Hall. Saint Thomas does hold a Tuesday evening concert series, but at $20–$50 I'd recommend keeping an eye out for the free choral music that happens during services.

Further uptown, the Broadway Presbyterian Church provides a stage and seating for a 45-piece chamber ensemble formed by amateur musicians serious about their hobbies. Despite the group's name, the Broadway Bach Ensemble chooses fall, winter, and spring programs that span a range from baroque to contemporary, so you're as likely to find Beethoven's Emperor Concerto as you are something obscure by Charles Ives. Nearby, you can hear the occasional orchestra and/or chamber concerts at Saint Paul's Chapel at Columbia by the New York Repertory Orchestra or the musicians from Juilliard. And the Cathedral of St. John the Divine is a jackpot of a performance venue, with everything from music to allegories brought to life, often for free. Not to be missed: Christmas Eve's Midnight Mass at St. John, whose proportions are no less than awe-inspiring.

BROADWAY BACH ENSEMBLE
Broadway Presbyterian Church
(Broadway @ 114th St.)
Upper West Side 914.654.1062

CATHEDRAL OF ST. JOHN THE DIVINE
1047 Amsterdam Ave. (@ 112th St.)
Upper West Side 212.662.2133

CHURCH OF THE HOLY APOSTLES
296 9th Ave. (@ 28th St.)
Chelsea 212.807.6799

SAINT PAUL'S CHAPEL–
COLUMBIA UNIVERSITY
Broadway (@ 116th St.)
Upper West Side 212.854.6256

SAINT PETER'S LUTHERAN CHURCH
619 Lexington Ave. (@ 54th St.)
Midtown 212.935.2200

SAINT THOMAS CHURCH
5th Ave. (@ 53rd St.)
Midtown 212.757.7013

TRINITY CHURCH
Broadway (@ Wall St.)
Financial District 212.602.0747

THE JUILLIARD SCHOOL OF MUSIC
65th St. (Broadway & Amsterdam Ave.)
Upper West Side 212.769.7406

Elite conservatories guarantee at least a modicum of excellence, and nowhere is this better proven than in the student and faculty performances at Juilliard. During the school year, a free event happens at least once a week. Classical music makes up the lion's share; several regular series populate the calendar: the five-event Sadenburg Faculty Recital Series, vocal arts debuts, the Juilliard Choral Union, the New Juilliard Ensemble, Juilliard Symphony (comprising sophomores and juniors), Juilliard Orchestra (seniors and first-year masters candidates), and pre-college Orchestra, Chamber Orchestra, and Symphony. During the day, a series called Wednesdays at One puts on a free weekly event involving chamber music, or a percussion ensemble, or solo organist. Where is there room for all this? Well, Lincoln Center's a treasure chest of venues, ranging from the intimate Paul Recital Hall to the bigger Juilliard Theater, up to the cavernous Alice Tully Hall and Avery Fisher Hall. Both fall and spring opera productions cost $20, still a deal compared to the Metropolitan. Although many performances are free, you might still have to pick up tickets in advance at the Juilliard box office. Call ahead to confirm availability.

MANNES COLLEGE OF MUSIC
150 W. 85th St. (Amsterdam & Columbus Aves.) Upper West Side 212.580.0210

Mannes is just another one of those exceptional music conservatories that occur in New York by the choirload. Mannes, founded in 1916 and recently subsumed by the New School, is known for a wide variety of instruments: Among the faculty are Elaine Doubas (oboist) and school dean Joel Lester (violinist). The 200-seat Mannes Concert Hall sees some 200+ student and faculty recitals throughout the school year that are typically free. Concerts with well-known visiting artists can cost nothing to $25; past artists have included flutist James Galway, pianists Charles Rosen and Jean-Yves Thibaudet, and violinist Ruggiero Ricci. The conductor of the Mannes Opera also conducts the City Opera and occasionally the Metropolitan Opera. In the summer, Mannes plays host to intensified workshops (including the Guitar Institute, Birth of Romanticism, and the renowned Keyboard Institute) in which you can find frequent master classes and performances for anywhere from the cost of an aborted cab ride to $20.

MANHATTAN SCHOOL OF MUSIC
120 Claremont Ave. (W. 122nd St. & Broadway) Upper West Side 212.749.2802

Why go to Lincoln Center, when you can go to Manhattan? There are usually no tickets to buy, as most of the student and faculty concerts are free. Performers are usually almost as amazing as the ones you'll find in professional orchestras, since the historic school makes up part of the talent pool the orchestras draw from.

LIBRARY FOR THE PERFORMING ARTS

40 LINCOLN CENTER PLAZA (@ BROADWAY)
UPPER WEST SIDE 212.870.1630

Leave your tux at home—here is one trip you can make to Lincoln Center without it. This branch of the New York Public Library—panacea for the masses who can't afford the tux or the tickets—puts on free performances throughout the year in its Bruno Walter Auditorium. Performances—which are sometimes linked to the library's curated gallery exhibits—are all over the map. One strand features distinguished musicians (conductor James Levine was on a recent schedule alongside folk singer Pete Seeger) and artists from the city's best companies (Metropolitan Opera, City Opera, City Ballet, and the Philharmonic). Another spotlights the creative process, bringing well-known composers, playwrights, and choreographers to talk about their work (heard of David Henry Hwang, or Elliott Carter?). There's also theater, dance, master classes—and none of this is limited to American art: The library is particularly proud of its global programming from places as far away as Japan and Kazakhstan. In accordance with the dress code (none), performances tend to be casual, replete with commentary from performers and happy, congratulatory words of introduction.

Unless you're a critic or a projectionist, it's not easy to see anything on the big screen for less than the $10 price of a ticket. But the more you try the better it gets: The selections off the beaten path are actually a lot richer than that tired blow-'em-up multiplex fare.

AMERICAN MUSEUM OF THE MOVING IMAGE
35th Ave. (@ 36th St.)
Astoria 718.784.4520

Located on the site of Paramount Studio's East Coast production studio from the 1920s, the AMMI is keeping its legacy very much alive. What a concept: There is a permanent exhibition at this museum with motion picture artifacts and the occasional lecture, but the happening "exhibits" are curated movies. Each one is a mini-festival you don't need a press pass to get into, just $10 ($7.50 for students; films are free with museum admission) and a few hours to kill. Once in, you can make a day of it, book-ending the films that play every Friday night and Saturday and Sunday afternoon with visits to the upstairs galleries. It's possible to catch a movie that hasn't yet made it into theaters, or is straight off the international festival circuit, and it wouldn't be unusual for a critic like J. Hoberman to introduce it. Fridays offer free admission to the gallery from

4pm-8pm. Note: If you're in the area, be sure to catch the museum's co-sponsored outdoor films at the Socrates Sculpture Park.

ANTHOLOGY FILM ARCHIVES
32 2nd Ave. (@ E. 2nd St.)
East Village 212.505.5181

If your definition of happiness includes watching on-camera eroticism with hubcaps, you might want to consider getting a membership at the Anthology. Once in a while, the Anthology plays host to the type of movies—commercially popular Korean films or Scandinavian horror—that flirt with urban mainstream. But invented by hippies and turned essential for today's cutting-edge moving-image artists, the Anthology is still the city's home of avant-garde and experimental cinema. Membership is comparatively cheap: Students join for $30, co-habiting couples $75, and the rest of us $50; from then on, members get either a free ride or pay the $5 student rate for a night's worth of downright weird entertainment.

IRIS AND B. GERALD CANTOR FILM CENTER
36 E. 8th St. (University Pl. & Greene St.)
East Village 212.998.4100

NYU's primary show space is big, pleasant, and comfortable, but the programming is done elsewhere, whether within or outside the university. Inside, it's really a grab bag: I've seen press screenings, films from mainland China, and films about S&M. Most of the movies are by invitation, but the Cantor Center opens its doors to the public about once a week. For programming information, look for flyers posted at the entrance, or call the main line and listen to the special events hotline.

NOTE: After you find out what you're seeing, you might need to pick your ticket up elsewhere.

OCULARIS AT GALAPAGOS
70 N. 6th St. (Wythe & Kent Aves.)
Williamsburg 718.388.8713

Ocularis began as a rooftop outdoor series for locals that screened movies to compete with the glittering Empire State Building. A few years later, the idea—which continues its outdoor summer series in various spots throughout Brooklyn and Queens—has moved into a more permanent spot in Galapagos' back room. The focus is on alternative, independent, and avant-garde cinema, and the frequently experimental selections range from mind-boggling to just plain weird—categories that are fortunately not mutually exclusive. $6 for an evening is the most you'll ever pay.

TWO BOOTS PIONEER THEATER
155 E. 3rd St. (@ Ave. A)
East Village 212.254.3300

When not playing host to any of a plethora of filmic urban resources (the Slamdance Film Festival, shorts festivals sponsored by the Independent Film Project, the East Village's Howl), this paean to independent cinema sprinkles its programming liberally with revivals and worthy second-run features. The theater itself—long, narrow, creaky, but not exactly uncomfortable—is exactly what comes to mind when you think of revival. On some nights, pay the usual $9 for the show, and grab a slice of steaming pizza first at the filmmakers' reception which takes place in the cleverly named Den of Cin, the shadowy lounge beneath the pizza joint next door.

DIRT CHEAP—NAH, FREE—VIDEO RENTALS

Blockbuster Video doesn't hold a candle to The Donnell Library Media Center. So long as you have a library card, you can borrow an unlimited number of videos and DVDs. The choice ranges from new feature film releases, to documentaries, to video art and the more experimental stuff typically carried by, say, Kim's. You don't have to stop with movies: The library has 35,000 recordings—including all kinds of music, foreign language instruction, books on tape—to fill your brain with. If you don't have a DVD player or a television set (bravo!), individual carrolls with screens are tucked behind door number one, the Film Video Study Center. The biggest dilemma may well be when to watch what you choose—you only have two weeks.

DONNELL LIBRARY MEDIA CENTER
20 W. 53rd St. (5th & 6th Aves.)
Midtown 212.621.0618

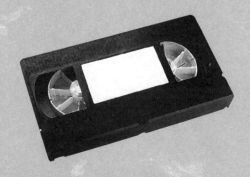

FLICKER NYC

I can't think of a better name for this monthly series of Super 8 and 16mm film. The projector whirs, casting the film in a soft, grainy glow. The image...flickers. There's no other way to describe it.

If you're at all nostalgic, even for a time you don't remember because you weren't born yet, you'd enjoy the NYC chapter of a nationwide series, curated by a single man with a humble passion. David Teague has found his favorite films in rummage sales, so home videos feature prominently, but Flicker also projects scripted film—it just depends. At Brooklyn's Barbes, which hosts the evening on alternate months, Teague's selection is accompanied by an improvising band or soloist. Think silent comedy.

Teague says, "One of my favorite films is an old home movie showing people dancing at an outdoor party. People young and old are swimming in the pool and just hanging out. I found it in the bottom of a box in a camera store in San Francisco, and the left side of the reel had been damaged, probably by oil or water, ruining the image on that side. So when you project film, the home movie footage breaks up into abstract colors every few seconds as the reel spins. It's really beautiful."

Tickets at The Knitting Factory are $5. At Barbes, shows are free with a suggested donation of $5.

FLICKER NYC
www.flickernyc.com

THE KNITTING FACTORY
75 Leonard St. (Church St. & Broadway)
TriBeCa 212.219.3055

BARBES
376 9th St. (@ 6th Ave.)
Park Slope 718.965.9177

STARS UNDER THE STARS

You are one lucky city dweller: Any day of the week in the summer, there are movies to see...and they're all gloriously free! Private and corporate sponsors have taken steps to quench the cinephile in every New Yorker; it's up to you to take advantage of it. One rule of thumb: Be considerate. I don't care how Herculean the effort necessary to restrain yourself from talking through the movie, or quoting all (but all!) the dialogue for the *Rocky Horror Picture Show*, but this looks nothing like your living room, and it's not, so can it.

BROOKLYN BRIDGE PARK SUMMER FILM SERIES
Empire/Fulton Ferry State Park
(Water St. bet. Main & New Dock Sts.)
DUMBO 718.802.0603

Approaching its fifth year, this fledgling festival is fast gaining the kind of popularity enjoyed by its long-standing counterpart in Bryant Park. Last year a single night in front of the big screen drew as many as 2,000 people, mostly Brooklynites, but also trekkers from the far-off reaches of the West Village and New Jersey. The popularity surely owes something to the programming—smart, campy originals like *Fargo* and *O Brother, Where Art Thou?*—but location's got to be the biggest factor. With nearly ten acres and a stunning backdrop, this venue makes watching an outdoor movie feel like a summer picnic, not a crowded elevator. You can hop a water taxi there, but why not walk or bike across the bridge and make the most of the glistening Manhattan skyline and East River. (A secure area provides bike storage.) Technically, you're supposed to leave your booze at home, but enforcement can be lax. Leave the dog at home, though: Pets are not allowed.

BRYANT PARK SUMMER FILM FESTIVAL
Bryant Park
(40th & 42nd Sts. bet. 5th & 6th Aves.)
Midtown www.bryantpark.org

The granddaddy of summer film festivals is offered on hot Monday nights. HBO sponsors this, and surprisingly, they like 'em old, so Bryant Park gives you the lovely, lilting classics—*American Graffiti, Planet of the Apes, Love Story, The Thin Man*. For these kind of crowds (10,000 was one estimate I got), get there as early as 5pm.

CELEBRATE BROOKLYN
Prospect Park Bandshell
(9th St. & Prospect Park West)
Prospect Park 718.855.7882

Celebrate Brooklyn is mostly a live performance outlet, but c'mon, you can't be serious about being an all-cultural summertime city fest until you break out the cinemascope. The wackier it gets the more turn out: One year they handed out 3-D glasses for *The Creature from the Black Lagoon*, and Brooklynites turned out in record numbers. Go figure.

Movies Under the Stars
Pier A Park
(East end of 1st St. @ Frank Sinatra Dr.)
Hoboken 201.420.2207

What started out as a homegrown production with a 16mm film projector and a mounted chunk of plywood has now graduated to a real screen, the centerpiece of a summer movie festival that can draw anywhere from 500 to 1,500 people. This is where you can go to watch recent blockbusters—*Love Actually*, *Seabiscuit*, and *School of Rock*—against the backdrop of the unencumbered Manhattan skyline. Grab a park bench or a city-provided chair (there are plenty to go around), or bring your own blanket or lawn chair. The sound system shares equipment with the venue's outdoor concerts. Plans for further expansion are in the works: Radio City Music Hall co-sponsored a mini Sinatra film festival in 2003.

River Flicks
Pier 54 (W. 14th St. & Hudson River)
Meatpacking District
Pier 25 (N. Moore St. & Hudson River)
TriBeCa 212.533.PARK

So what if you're not wild about the unimpeded view of the New Jersey skyline? You're a lazy Manhattanite, and you know you don't have far to travel to Pier 54 (W. 14th St.) on Wednesdays, and Pier 25 (N. Moore St.) on Fridays. And besides, you're here for the movies.

And some movies they are. 1980s and 1990s blockbusters such as *Goodfellas* take up the bulk of the two programs, but once in a while an indie hit like *My Big Fat Greek Wedding* will pop up on the menu (this is not the time to practice saying "boont cake"). My advice is to get as close to the screen as possible—sometimes the glare from the water, and the light of dusk, will throw off your vision. Unless of course you are there for the view.

ROOFTOP FILMS
Various locations; check www.rooftop-films.com or call 877.786.1912
for additional information

This is the urban equivalent of a drive-in movie experience when (a) you have no car, and (b) the movies look less like crowd-pleasers and more like intellectual art house thinkfare (foreign shorts and the like). The similarities are that you go in summer, pay $7 to get in, and once there you can make-out all you want. Oh yeah, and with lots of space, this roof isn't likely to sell out.

You don't outgrow storytelling simply by trading the Berenstein Bears for the Babysitters Club. Think of it as city s'mores, with a crowd savvier than a bunch of Girl or Boy Scouts, nevertheless collectively transfixed by a single voice. Don't like being read to? Then get on stage…certain forums tend to be pretty democratic.

ARLENE GROCERY
95 Stanton St. (Ludlow & Orchard Sts.)
Lower East Side 212.358.1633

This little piece of real estate has gone from a family-owned grocery store with questionable produce, to a dank and seedy rock venue, to its current renovated digs, home to live bands, punk rock karaoke with a following…and poetry readings. Check the times, but the readings are usually on Sundays.

BARBES
376 9th St. (@ 6th Ave.)
Park Slope 718.965.9177

This hip Brooklyn bar and music joint gives occasional billing to artists of the written word. Check out the regular readings from the folks who bring you *McSweeney's*, typically free. For a more complete description of the venue, see Rock Cheap.

BARNES & NOBLE BOOKSELLERS
Various locations throughout NYC, including:

240 E. 86th St. (@ 2nd Ave.)
Upper East Side 212.794.1962

1280 Lexington Ave. (@ 86th St.)
Upper East Side 212.423.9900

2289 Broadway (@ 82nd St.)
Upper West Side 212.362.8835

1972 Broadway (@ Lincoln Center)
Upper West Side 212.595.6859

160 E. 54th St. (@ Citigroup Center)
Midtown 212.750.8033

600 5th Ave. (@ Rockefeller Center)
Midtown 212.765.0592

750 3rd Ave. (@ 47th St.)
Midtown 212.697.2251

675 6th Ave. (@ 22nd St.)
Chelsea 212.727.1227

33 E. 17th St. (@ Union Sq. North)
Flatiron 212.253.0810

4 Astor Pl. (Broadway & 4th Ave.)
Greenwich Village 212.420.1322

396 6th Ave. (@ 8th St.)
West Village 212.674.8780

106 Court St. (Schermerhorn & State Sts.)
Brooklyn 718.246.4996

Oh, but it's so much more than a large, corporate bookstore chain. I know people who eat their lunches solely in the Starbucks within. Or kick up their music collections via the listening stations posted throughout the CD section. And it's entirely conceivable that you'll meet your future spouse in the travel section while contemplating a trip to Brunei.

Consider the readings—which happen daily at each of the numerous stores—an extension of the literary vibe-fest. Sit back and listen to authors read from their own work, and try your best to disregard the sound of the cash registers in the background. Afterwards: Q&A, and an opportunity to meet the story's real hero—the writer.

BOWERY POETRY CLUB
308 Bowery (Bleecker & Houston Sts.)
East Village 212.614.0505

This dark but not quite dingy club encapsulates the essence of an urban performance space where anything truly goes. Certainly, a dedication to the oral tradition is at the center of it all, with Poetry Slams, literary panels, balladeering bands, and expressive roundtable readings for anywhere from free to $15. Crowds are scant, or intimate in the back room, or occasionally spill out onto the Bowery. The café also sells coffee and sandwiches, which get discounted every evening.

CORNELIA STREET CAFÉ
29 Cornelia St. (Bleecker & W. 4th Sts.)
West Village 212.989.9319

It's quite a thing to be huddled over a well-crafted poem, while you're actually sitting upright at a teensy table a good distance from the nearest fellow listener. But that's exactly the feeling given by this cozy subterranean space when the room is filled and the story/essay/poem is good. There may be a small cover, but that is small penance for being in the coveted spot, especially when you're hungry—the food lives up to the great reputation of the restaurant upstairs.

KGB BAR
85 E. 4th St. (2nd & 3rd Aves.)
East Village 212.505.3360

They don't call it the KGB just to be cute: The bar was home to the Ukrainian Communist Party's U.S. headquarters. Now it's home to revolutionaries of a less politicized shade of red, hosting free fiction, non-fiction, and poetry readings most nights starting at 7pm. Stay for drinks (no draft beers, but there is a full bar) and cognoscenti-type banter until 4am.

THE KNITTING FACTORY
75 Leonard St. (Church St. & Broadway)
TriBeCa 212.219.3055

That very same live music legend stows away a miniature venue where poets do regularly gather. It's usually something eminently reasonable (free, $5) to get in.

THE LIVING ROOM
154 Ludlow St. (Stanton & Rivington Sts.)
Lower East Side 212.533.7235

The new Living Room has a glowing orange aura, with poets and writers reading from works of fiction and anthologies once a month.

THE MOTH
Various venues in Manhattan and Brooklyn
www.themoth.org

Once upon a time a boy from Georgia sat awash in the heat of a Deep South summer, captivated by the stories of his friends and neighbors. The boy grew up to be a man, and the man, a poet and novelist named George Dawes Green, moved to NYC and founded The Moth. The series is so named because the central characters of the stories that Green remembers did not have happy endings; they would always get burned and then, like moths, return stubbornly—and stupidly—to the flame. Unlike those moths, though, this one has taken colorful flight, drawing name actors and big crowds in various Manhattan and Brooklyn venues (three that illustrate the diversity: City Hall, the Nuyorican Poets Café, and the American Museum of Natural History). There are several events of note. The first and pricier, a themed evening called Stories at the Moth ($20), screens and workshops pre-submitted stories for presentation before a live audience. Forget reality: The Moth encourages exaggeration, "to provide a more meaningful experience for the audience." During these nights, volunteers may improve with audience suggestions. The second notable event is the themed StorySLAM ($6), in which 10 willing audience members chosen at random get the stage for five minutes, after which they're scored by a jury of their peers. It's usually rollicking entertainment.

Nuyorican Poets Café
236 E. 3rd St. (Aves. B & C)
East Village 212.505.8183

The "Nuyorican" in the name was taken from a poetry anthology published by William Morrow in the 1970s. But what started as a group of Nuyorican poets gathering to read their work in a college professor's living room grew to embrace a multicultural concept which now includes prose, hip-hop, visual arts, music, comedy, screenplay readings, and theater. Of special note: the weekly Poetry Slams, judged by random people from the audience, and Thursdays' Latin Jazz Jam Sessions.

STRAND BOOK STORE
828 Broadway (@ 12th St.)
Greenwich Village 212.473.1452

95 Fulton St. (@ Gold St.),
Financial District 212.732.6070

45 W. 57th St., 5th Fl. (5th & 6th Aves.)
Midtown 212.688.7600

Strand Book Store makes the curious claim of housing "eight miles of books"—and they speak the truth. Founded in 1927 and named for both London's famous publishing street and an old literary magazine, Strand has remained a family business known worldwide as the place to get the best deals on any book under the sun. Strand features the largest rare book collection in New York City, including an impressive assortment of hard-to-find art and photography books. Be sure to peruse the outdoor bin—a perfect spot to find interesting reading at unbelievably low prices.

THE NEW YORKER FESTIVAL

In 1999, the venerated literary magazine introduced a three-day weekend in autumn to give live audiences a chance to meet and listen to authors, scholars, and journalists. The festival—a city-wide salon as spicy and thought-provoking as the magazine itself—was a hit from the get-go. Since then, the likes of Jonathan Franzen and Dave Eggers have been joined by filmmakers (Martin Scorsese and the Coen brothers), musicians (Aimee Mann and Tracey Chapman), politicians (Kofi Annan), and other performers (Matt Dillon, Eddie Izzard, and others). Upwards of 40,000 have swarmed to the various events. Most significantly, the readings—like rock concerts—sell out within hours. Day one is generally Fiction Night: two authors sharing their work at each of two separate "seatings" in various venues around town (none of them are big enough—these are the events that sell out the quickest). Day two is typically dedicated to non-fiction, and filled with conversations and panels between and among journalists and commentators: sort of like live NPR. Day three, dedicated to your city, comprises walking tours by staff writers and contributors: Adam Gopnik tours Harlem, Calvin Trillin shows you Chinatown. Tickets run $15 and up; at some events, the festival gives out sponsor-bought popcorn and candy.

Note: If authors are not your rock stars, know that not everything requires a ticket:

The festival is dotted with free events, like the opportunity to watch a movie with Anthony Lane. Authors' book signings– always free–fill up two days at festival headquarters, the Barnes & Noble in Union Square.

Just because you've already got your degree is no reason to let your brain rot to a slow death in the nearest corner pub. New York may be an education in and of itself, but classes in New York still abound, from the sublime to the downright wacky. Despite the rising cost of education, we've found some for which you won't have to skip a month's rent.

THE ART STUDENTS LEAGUE
215 W. 57th St. (7th Ave. & Broadway)
Midtown 212.247.4510

Suspect that a Vincent or a Georgia lurks beneath all your stick doodling? Let The Art Students League confirm your suspicions. The classes—such as Anatomy for Artists and Printmaking—are cleverly organized by availability for students (i.e., two evenings, five mornings, etc.) and run as low as $59 for one night a week for a month.

BROOKLYN CONSERVATORY OF MUSIC
58 7th Ave. (@ Lincoln Pl.)
Park Slope 718.622.3300

42–76 Main St (@ Northern Blvd.)
Flushing 718.461.8910

If you've always wanted to learn how to sing, then consider taking a class at the Brooklyn Conservatory. With two locations, the school offers instruction at a completely amateur and beginning level in voice, piano, orchestral, and jazz instruments. The one-on-one private lessons are only $34 for each 30-minute lesson purchased in a 16-week series.

THE EDUCATIONAL ALLIANCE ART SCHOOL
197 E. Broadway (Jefferson & Clinton Sts.) Lower East Side
212.780.2300 ext. 428

Turn to the Art School at the Lower East Side's Educational Alliance to learn how to fire killer ceramics and shoot gallery-quality photographs. Once you've paid your annual registration fee of $60, 12-session courses run anywhere from $30 per class, to the all-time bargain basement price of $12.50 (lab fees are extra, but not much). You get polite instructors, free studio time, and a brand new hobby, all with money left over to buy stuff to support it (camera, brushes, paint...).

GOTHAM WRITERS' WORKSHOP
Various locations in NYC
www.writingclasses.com

The Gotham Writers' Workshop bills itself as America's leading school for creative writing. It'll take about $400 (for the 10-week course) to become a full-fledged novelist...but pay attention. You can also go to the hour-long lectures given for free at various bookstores across town. These are held by Gotham's rotating stable of writers: for the most part—well-published, working writers who are not household names, but nevertheless talented and able to bring the topic to life. Of course they're going to urge you to sign up for the paid courses. And if you're serious about tackling the craft, you'll shell out the money.

THE HENRY GEORGE SCHOOL
121 E. 30th St. (Lexington Ave. & Park Ave. South) Murray Hill 212.889.8020

For activists who lie awake stressing over rampant homelessness, here's a different remedy. Henry George was a leftist reformer, and you can carry on his tradition: At The Henry George School of Social Science, not only will you learn why social problems occur, but also what you can do about it. Classes—appropriately enough—are always free.

JEWISH COMMUNITY CENTER
The Samuel Priest Rose Building
334 Amsterdam Ave. (@ W. 76th St.)
Upper West Side 646.505.4444

Films, lectures, pre-holiday workshops, book discussion groups, kosher wine classes—if it has to do with Judaism or with educating or improving the community, it is likely to be free or to cost very little money ($15 per event and under) at the JCC. Come join 16,000 Jews and non-Jews, members, and non-members in a jewel of an Upper West Side building. When appropriate, events are conveniently divided into age categories.

KATE'S PAPERIE
561 Broadway (@ Prince St.)
SoHo 212.941.9816

8 W. 13th St. (5th & 6th Aves.)
Greenwich Village 212.633.0570

1282 3rd Ave. (73rd & 74th Sts.)
Upper East Side 212.396.3670

140 W. 57th St. (6th & 7th Aves.)
Midtown 212.459.0700

So maybe scrunching up against 399 strangers in a busy retail store isn't your idea of a great way to spend a crisp autumn evening. Think again: What if your two-hour-long sacrifice taught you how to make an exquisite gift basket? Think of the possibilities—and the savings—at holidays, birthdays, anniversaries, and christenings. Never been much of a gift giver? You'll astound.

The specialty paper goods emporium—recently expanded to five locations, including one in Greenwich, CT—hosts demonstrations at all stores. In addition to gift baskets, you'll learn card-making and gift-wrapping skills that'll have you swatting away requests from friends in no time. In April, the cherry blossoms inspire how-tos involving origami, brush-painting, and Japanese floral arrangements. Keep in mind that these are demonstrations, not hands-on classes. If you get hooked, you can sign up for those as well: For $60 (materials included), you'll go home with a handful of cards and a generous lifetime hobby.

NOTE: Keep your eyes peeled for the do-it-yourself wedding events (come even just for free wedding cake by celebrity baker Martin Howard).

THE NEW SCHOOL
66 W. 12th St. (5th & 6th Aves.)
West Village 212.229.5353

If you're not one to spend a lot of money at the 92nd Street Y, but would still like not to be left out in the cold during earnest panel discussions about the health of our nation's Bill of Rights, you've come to the right place. For $25 and up (lectures, readings, and screenings are often free), you can learn much at the bohemian Village institution, The New School. The programs have a policy-political bias, but the programs aren't all serious: One wacky installment featured a slide show about one man's voyage around the world on a 40-foot sailboat. Sometimes there is a catch: maybe a CFA's trying to sell you her services under the guise of advice on mutual funds, or one of the adjunct professors is raising hype for a more expensive, 13-session class. Regardless, you're still going to drum up some excitement in your cortex, even if the knowledge you gain is simply that you need to know more.

THE NEW YORK OPEN CENTER
83 Spring St. (Broadway & Lafayette St.)
SoHo 212.219.2527

Maybe you're fascinated with the principles of feng shui, or you want to be a reflexologist. The New York Open Center can introduce you to these disciplines for free before you commit to taking a multiple-session course. The loft building across the street from Balthazar is a goldmine of all things spiritual—beyond classes, the center holds art shows, concerts (New Age drumming, anyone?), and wellness treatments from $50-$65 an hour. Most of the classes are more experiential than they are technical: If you're taking photography, you'll focus more on shooting by intuition than you will on which aperture settings to use. The Center is firm on this point: Talent's not necessary—this is one place where you can paint stick figures in peace.

SCHOOL OF PRACTICAL PHILOSOPHY
12 E. 79th St. (5th & Madison Aves.)
Upper East Side 212.744.4848

If you're reading this book, you have more dreams than money. So pass over a night course at NYU in favor of an evening session for $30 at the School of Practical Philosophy. The topics—chosen and taught by former students completely gratis (other cash-strapped dreamers; see a trend?)—are pretty esoteric, running the gamut from where Shakespeare got his mojo (language, in this context) to the history of philosophy.

You could spend hard-earned dinner money getting into the city museums if you pay what they ask for. On the other hand, you could be smart and spend nothing at all. Follow these tips for getting your art fix for next to nothing.

MUSEUM OF TELEVISION AND RADIO
25 W. 52nd St. (5th & 6th Aves.)
Midtown 212.621.6600

This rhymes with—and should be called—the Museum of the Couch Potato. Notwithstanding that founder William S. Paley (chairman and founder of CBS) was himself no couch slouch, there is little option here but to park your behind and stare at one of many state-of-the-art screens. The Museum of the Stuffed Tomato ($10 to get in, $8 for senior citizens and full-time students, free for members) has several console centers with individual screen and headset setups, a few theaters and screening rooms, galleries with moving and still exhibitions, a radio studio, and the vast collection, which houses over 120,000 American and foreign programs, including—of course—almost everything produced or broadcast by CBS.

GIVE NOT WANT NOT: GETTING IN FREE TO MUSEUMS

It's true that museums run the money they get from attendees back into their operating budgets. But it's also true that the museums which ask for suggested donations typically already get money from the City of New York—via the taxes you pay. So whenever you see a "suggested" donation, feel free to pay as little as $1. The following is a list of some of these museums:

METROPOLITAN MUSEUM OF ART
1000 5th Ave. (@ 82nd St.)
Upper East Side 212.535.7710

MUSEUM OF THE CITY OF NEW YORK
1220 5th Ave. (@ 103rd St.)
Upper East Side 212.534.1672

NEW YORK CITY FIRE MUSEUM
278 Spring St. (Hudson & Varick Sts.)
SoHo 212.691.1303

P.S. 1 CONTEMPORARY ART CENTER
22-25 Jackson Ave. (@ 46th Ave.)
Long Island City 718.784.2084

MUSEUM MILE FESTIVAL

From 6pm-9pm on the second Tuesday in June, the nine museums on Museum Mile (5th Ave., 82nd to102nd Sts.) open their doors to the throngs for free. Best to go early; in 2003, 50,000 people showed up. Of the nine, the two biggies are the Metropolitan (stretching from 82nd to 86th Sts.) and the Guggenheim (88th St.). Wanna shoot for a marathon? The rest of the museums are: El Museo del Barrio (104th St.), Museum of the City of New York (103rd St.), International Center of Photography (94th St.), Jewish Museum (92nd St.), Cooper-Hewitt National Museum of Design (91st St.), National Academy Museum and School of Fine Arts (89th St.), and the Goethe House Cultural Center (83rd St.). For more information, call 212.606.2296 or visit www.museummilefestival.org.

FREE/PAY WHAT YOU WISH NIGHT

If being single has somehow come to relate to being dirt cheap, then this is probably the greatest informal singles night out in all of NYC. Come one, come all to mingle and flirt. Art? Yes, that too. But first hand me another cracker with cheese, please.

AMERICAN FOLK ART MUSEUM
45 W. 53rd St. (5th & 6th Aves.)
Midtown 212.922.7170
Fri. 5:30pm–7:30pm

ASIA SOCIETY
725 Park Ave. (@ 70th St.)
Upper East Side 212.288.6400
Fri. 6pm–9pm

INTERNATIONAL CENTER OF PHOTOGRAPHY
1133 6th Ave. (@ 43rd St.)
Midtown 212.857.0000
Fri. 5pm–8pm

JEWISH MUSEUM
1109 5th Ave. (@ 92nd St.)
Upper East Side 212.423.3200
Thurs. 5pm–8pm

MUSEUM OF MODERN ART
33rd St. (@ Queens Blvd.)
Long Island City 212.708.9400
Fri. 4pm–7:45pm

SOLOMON R. GUGGENHEIM MUSEUM
1071 5th Ave. (@ 89th St.)
Upper East Side 212.423.3500
Fri. 6pm–8pm

WHITNEY MUSEUM OF AMERICAN ART
945 Madison Ave. (@ 75th St.)
Upper East Side 212.570.3600
Fri. 6pm–9pm

NEWHOUSE CENTER FOR CONTEMPORARY ART

Snug Harbor Cultural Center
1000 Richmond Terrace, Bldg. C
Staten Island 718.448.2500 ext. 260

Snug Harbor is everything the name conjures: a neat row of Greek revival mansions overlooking the water with Manhattan and Lady Liberty in the backdrop. The best news of all: This museum is only $2 to get into ($1 for senior citizens, and free for members and children under 10).

QUEENS MUSEUM OF ART

New York City Building
Flushing Meadows Corona Park
Flushing 718.592.9700

You've just got to love a city where a borough that takes flack for not being sufficiently cultural is home to an art museum that would culturalize the pants off of most cities. And I'm not talking about the MoMA. Not far from Shea Stadium, the Queens Museum of Art is the last surviving structure built expressly for the 1939 World's Fair. The so-called "New York City Building" houses an interesting history: After World War II, it became U.N. headquarters until the General Assembly moved across the East River. The building then hosted another World's Fair (1964), which led logically to its transformation into a museum whose largest permanent exhibits are displays from both World's Fairs, including the gargantuan Panorama of the City of New York, a 9,335-square-foot replica, updated and refurbished and with new lights for a glorious nightscape view. And another oldie but goodie, on extended loan to the museum: a private collection of Tiffany glass and lamps. Good temporary exhibits also rotate in and out of here, such as the recent visual recall of Salvador Dali's "Dream of Venus," an installation that appeared in—you guessed it—the World's Fair. There is a suggested donation of $5.

FIRST SATURDAYS, AFTER-HOURS FREE MUSEUM PARTY

Museums typically close at 5pm or 6pm, so it is the rare evening you get to cavort in one after dark. But the Brooklyn Museum—the same institution that created a recent scandal for exhibiting a Madonna painting with elephant dung—wants you to come to the nighttime party it throws on the first Saturday of every month (except September, when the West Indian Festival takes over the space) from 5pm-11pm.

In its first five years, First Saturday has gotten a phenomenal response. In 2003, 10,000 people showed up to celebrate Mardi Gras. (It's a spacious museum, but sheesh—kudos to the organizers for improvising.) Luckily, the Beaux-Art Court is a sizeable old-fashioned ballroom with 19th-century European paintings hanging on the walls. But First Saturdays is less about ballroom dancing, and more about an eclectic mix of bands that range from klezmer to Afro beats, old-time hillbilly to alternative rock. Oh, and I almost forgot: glorious art.

BROOKLYN MUSEUM OF ART
200 Eastern Pkwy. (@ Washington Ave.)
Park Slope 718.638.5000

THE GREATEST FREE ART SHOWS IN NYC

Question: In what public place can you find—and touch—a priceless vase from the Ming Dynasty?

Simple—an auction house. Whether a house is a multinational conglomerate like Sotheby's or a private East Coast venture like Doyle, the house philosophy is always the same: Let the potential bidder (i.e., you) interact with the lots (i.e., the art). Therefore you'll never find a velvet rope or a glass case in one of these "museums," just friendly, helpful attendants required to treat you as a bidder-to-be.

Whether you're interested in cars, furniture, or paintings, auctions are once-in-a-lifetime opportunities to see collections of precious magnitude before the works get scattered to the four winds.

Most of the auction houses listed below have elaborately detailed websites where you can preview goods before arriving on the block. Just don't get accustomed to being so up close and personal.

CHRISTIE'S
20 Rockefeller Plaza (@ 49th St.)
Midtown 212.636.2000

This 310,000-square-foot branch of the old auction house, which welcomes visitors with a soaring triple-height mural, knows few limits. With select summer auctions and 35 sales during each of the fall, winter, and spring, Christie's is like a museum jumped up with Red Bull. Everything is fair game here: You're likely to find antique cars which borrow the wide plazas of Rockefeller Center, as well as exquisite art. When *Playboy* turned 50, Hugh Hefner sold his correspondence here, along with a few bunny costumes, soft porn cartoons, and *Playboy*-published writings by the likes of Jack Kerouac.

DOYLE NEW YORK

175 E. 87th St. (Lexington & 3rd Aves.)
Upper East Side 212.427.2730

The number one place in the world to auction important vintage couture is located in a building that turns into a fantasy fashion retrospective once or twice a year, previewing 150 years of stunning original clothing.

Couture isn't the only thing sold at Doyle. The house holds 30–40 auctions in 13 different categories every year, including European and American paintings, rare books and autographs, prints, antique furniture, and celebrity estates. In 2003, Doyle housed the most important collection of porcelain from the Ming Dynasty ever gathered in a single spot.

Doyle also makes auctions accessible to the public, offering a free monthly class Sunday mornings about how to buy at auctions. It's really not as Hollywood as it all seems.

PHILLIPS AUCTION HOUSE
450 W. 15th St. (9th & 10th Aves.)
Chelsea 212.940.1200

With its digs in art-friendly Chelsea, this small New York auction house specializes in art. The definition of art can be stretched—it wouldn't be far-fetched to spot an Eames chair in here, for example, but you'll find little in the way of antiques (i.e. stamps or coins) and don't expect to peer into any car windows. As with its bigger competitors, auctions and previews are open to the public—there are fewer sales and only one floor for viewing. But during the auctions, bidding can get competitive and anxiety-ridden. Expect to see a few black horses...and bring popcorn.

SOTHEBY'S
1334 York Ave. (@ 72nd St.)
Upper East Side 212.606.7000

In its 250-year history, the British auction house has sold and displayed everything in the fine and decorative art world from Napoleon's book collection, to the Duchess of Windsor's jewels, to Lulu Guinness' cartoon-like handbags—which may get interpreted eventually as our modern-day hieroglyphics (hey, you never know). The institution's astounding volume—which hit $2 billion in recent years—is on a crazy hot-air balloon ride that has even expanded in recent troubled times. Yeah, yeah, you mutter, but what's in it for the average Joe who can't afford a picture? The answer is simple—the New York office could almost double as a museum, but one that doesn't charge a cent and offers the possibility of taking something home (although for that, consult a different book). Collections go on public display a full week in advance of the auctions. Viewing is best in the dramatic tenth floor gallery: The space has been compared more favorably against some of the city's top museums. The auctions themselves are free entertainment.

WITH OVER 1,450 BARS REVIEWED,
SHECKY'S STAFF DAMAGES THEIR LIVERS
SO YOU DON'T HAVE TO

SHECKY'S

BAR, CLUB & LOUNGE GUIDE

2005 NEW YORK

OVER 1450 HOT SPOTS!

FOX 5's "GOOD DAY NEW YORK" CALLS IT
THE NIGHTLIFE BIBLE"

**SHECKY'S BAR, CLUB & LOUNGE
GUIDE 2005 NEW YORK**

**IN STORES EVERYWHERE
SEPTEMBER 25TH**

4 PLAY *cheap*

We've made you pretty, we've given you culture. Now we'll cut straight to the chase—it's time to fix your love life. If you're lonely, there are thousands of bars and a few parties out there to help you find a date—and you don't have to spend a lot of money to do it. If you're hooked up, then this chapter will help the two of you keep all four hands firmly on your respective wallets. We'll show you how to woo the future love of your life on a pauper's budget, plus tell you where to get your food and

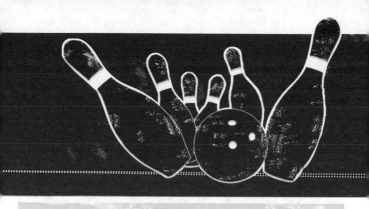

drink on when money is a consideration (did somebody say happy hour?). Show your date your playful side by enjoying a bargain baseball game (Yankees, Schmankees), a sultry night of dancing, a romantic trip to the Brooklyn Botanic Garden, or a heated game of backgammon. Love doesn't cost a thing, and this chapter will show you why.

In a perfect world, there is unlimited money to be spent on the eating, drinking, and viewing pleasure of a couple of kids on their merry way to "I do," a scenario which typically runs about $250 per glittery evening. But let's face it: Life in the aftermath of "I do" is a lot more pleasant without a mass of credit card debt. (Ladies, you want your guy to be frugal, right? Right?) This section is dedicated to making couples happy…in the long term.

HURRYDATE
Various locations in NYC
www.hurrydate.com

Think of it this way: you're getting 25 dates for the all-time bargain price of $37 (for non-members)…up to 30 three- to six-minute dates. If this sounds nerve-racking to you (memories of rush, job interviews, that essential presentation come flooding back—you're good under pressure right?), wait until that hottie that caught your eye at the door lands across the desk. Work it, work it.

FIRST DATE: The Iris and B. Gerald Cantor Roof Garden

METROPOLITAN MUSEUM OF ART
5th Ave. (@ 82nd St.)
Upper East Side 212.535.7710

If you have high hopes about a brand-new date, raise them up onto the pedestal where they belong. The top of the Metropolitan Museum houses a manicured garden overlooking both Central Park and the twinkling skyline. Obliterate your first-date awkwardness under the pretense of gazing at the star-lined panorama. In the alternative, feed your art jinks: Installations by name-brand artists like Roy Lichtenstein add a nice bonus to that dizzying view.

DAY DATE: Coney Island

ASTROLAND
1000 Surf Ave. (@ W. 10th St.)
Coney Island 718.372.0275

First-date jitters seem like a memory already, and you and your new S.O.-in-training are moving rapidly into the sweet beginnings of coupledom. No better time to treat yourself to a little flirtation…between bumper cars.

The W train to the last stop is an easy journey into the past…about 100 years. They call it NYC's largest amusement park, but Astroland really is NYC's only amusement park. Its innocence is still personified: Play pranks on her in Dante's Inferno (the haunted house), make him win you a giant stuffed animal, laugh together at the size of the splash at the end of the water flume ride.

The world-famous Cyclone is here: still made of wood, still rickety, still twisting, and still scary. Other rides hit major bases: the happiness of the swings, the stomach-drop of the swinging pirate ship, the dizziness of the spinning tea cups, and The Enterprise—a disc that whirls you upside-down and backwards so that afterwards, you defy gravity.

There are two pricing options, depending on when you go. Get there on a weekday, and you can pay $21.99 for an unlimited number of rides during a six-hour session, and $17.99 if you skip the Cyclone (but then, what's the point?); take that, Six Flags Great Adventure. On Friday nights, weekends, and holidays, there ain't no such beast…but it's still cheap and even more retro: You buy $2-$5 ride coupons, and tear them off as you go.

After you're done spinning yourself into another solar system, you might want to consider checking out the nearby attractions. The beach and boardwalk are a stone's throw away and both are free. Admission to a museum with Coney Island memorabilia—worth absorbing even if you're not a history buff—is only $1. When hunger calls, skip the dog and go for an authentic piero-gi. Walk down Brighton Beach Boulevard to the famed Russian enclave, Brighton Beach, also known as Little Odessa by the Sea. There are about a half-dozen "restorans," nightclubs mas-querading as restaurants, where every day is like New Year's Eve or a wedding. The restorans stage Vegas-like acts accompanied by banquets (who really eats like this?) and copious bottles of liquid smoke (vodka); avoid them. It might be an interesting way to get to know your date, but unless you're a super-duper vodka athlete, you're just going to blow a lot of money (about $80/per-son) and hurt yourself. For a filling meal try Primorski, which usu-ally has live music. Or simply buy a few pirozhkis—Russian meat pies—from a streetside kiosk. Or make a stop at M & I International Foods (249 Brighton Beach Ave.), where you can get cut-rate caviar, sausages, smoked fish, and wrapped Russian chocolates—rich, smooth, and gargantuan.

THE OVERNIGHT DATE: City Island, Bronx

When you're ready to fly to the next lily pad in the sky, we have an idea for where to put your fuzzy-in-love heads. The name City Island is what makes Bronxites perk up: Why, don't you also have your own private Nantucket? What they know is that the last stop on the 6 (Pelham Bay Park) leads to a quaint little seaport enclave dotted with lighthouses and smeared with crab shacks and sand. A half-hour from toe to tip, City Island is teensy enough to feel provincial, without the snot-nosed crowds of say the haughty Hamptons.

Once out of the subway, cross over the long access bridge and transfer to the BX29 bus going to City Island. The bus trip takes less than 10 minutes to the City Island Bridge and about 15 minutes to the end of City Island. Another option is to walk the 40 minutes through Pelham Bay Park. After the bridge, bear right, following the signs to the City Island Bridge.

As you enter the island you see a few seafood restaurants and boat slips. Check into Le Refuge, the island's bargain bed and breakfast ($85 for a double), then go antiquing with the money you saved not having to truck all the way up the coast (there's a decent vintage record store midway down the street). For dinner, take your pick: You can get lobsters with all the fixings  for about $15 and up at either Crab Shanty or Johnny's Reef, the last restaurant on the main drag facing away from the bridge. At the southern end is a pseudo-food court, where you can pick up fried seafood for a little makeshift picnic.

LE REFUGE BED & BREAKFAST
620 City Island Ave. (@ Bridge St.)
City Island 718.885.2478

Manhattan chef Pierre Saint-Denis bought this 19th-century Victorian mansion, which a sea captain used to call home. Saint-Denis named it Le Refuge, after his Upper East Side Manhattan restaurant. What's in there: seven large bedrooms, including three king bed suites with private bathrooms. Make time for smooching.

DIY GIFTS THAT REQUIRE LITTLE IN THE WAY OF TALENT

If you like the idea of DIY, but are resolutely non-crafty, take a hint from a fellow non-DIY-er: Never lose sight of your limitations. For a housewarming gift for your new sweetie, one great idea that's more PITY (put-it-together-yourself) than DIY is a wok filled with all the non-perishable items needed for a stir-fry. Stuff it to the brim with dried egg noodles, a bottle of oyster sauce, a mini tin of soy sauce, a package of dried shiitake mushrooms, a can of bamboo shoots, and a recipe printout. Add julienned strips of carrot and fresh chicken and voila: chicken chow mein. Or you can buy a cheap orchid in either the Flower District (28th Street around 6th Avenue) or the Astor Place K-Mart, and upgrade it yourself to a more expensive ceramic pot with a huge ribbon around the base. If you're hungry for more and getting the knack of it, burn your own CD with a theme: sexy lounge music, '80s, James Bond; if you've got a digital camera you can always stick a picture of the recipient—or yourself—on the cover.

Increasing numbers of happy hours are one result of these downtrodden times. It seems every bar's got a scheme—and they all want your warm butt. In this section, you'll find beer specials, cocktail specials, cheap wine, and great free food.

CHEAP BEER, COCKTAILS, AND WINE

AUTOMATIC SLIMS
733 Washington St. (@ Bank St.)
West Village 212.645.8660

The unique glass-top tables displaying dominos or old 45s and the creative menu and checker-board floor set this bar apart from others in the West Village. Another surprise: a kitchen that turns out distinctively non-bar selections like a $7 warm goat cheese salad, a $5 fresh cheese quesadilla, and $16 filet mignon. After hours, Automatic takes on the mystique of a nightclub. But you want to come for the Monday-Saturday happy hour, serving $4 well drinks and $3 drafts and bottles (including Stella) from 5:30pm-8pm.

BAR EAST
1733 1st Ave. (@ 90th St.)
Upper East Side 212.876.0203

Go east, young man and grab yourself some beer! A laid-back neighborhood spot with ample space to put your feet up, Bar East is what everyone needs after a long day of brownnosing and social climbing. They've got eight beers on tap served up in $2 pints, three televisions, two pool tables, a dartboard, and a drunk in the bathroom. Can your living room beat that? Although guest bartenders are always welcome and a DJ plays music Thursday through Saturday nights, there is never a cover charge nor is there going to be a problem finding seats for you and that horde of hellions you call friends.

BENNY'S BURRITOS (EAST)
93 Ave. A (@ E. 6th St.)
East Village 212.254.2054

BENNY'S BURRITOS (WEST)
113 Greenwich Ave. (Jane & W. 12th Sts.)
West Village 212.727.3560

Although they have different owners, these two spots have a lot in common: Both hug a popular corner, both serve creative Mexican food, both have kicking happy hours, both have a way of spilling over with afternoon-to-evening revelers. In the West Village, the daily draw is from 4pm-7pm, for the $4 margaritas (reg. $6), $6.50-$7.50 for the two-person grande margaritas (the size of a half carafe, reg. $10), and $2.50 Rolling Rocks. The East Village version goes on sale from 4pm-7pm and also 10pm-11pm, with free chips and salsa and cheaper drinks, probably a reflection of a more bohemian customer base; the margaritas and well drinks cost just $3.

BLEECKER STREET BAR
58 Bleecker St. (@ Crosby St.)
NoHo 212.334.0244

We all know happy hour's never really an hour long. At this NoHo dive, they really do believe in happiness—to the tune of an official, eight-hour work day. From noon-8pm, get a 24-oz. Miller Lite Draft for only $3.50. Hey, eight hours would fly for you at work, too, if you had three pool tables, three dartboards, a jukebox, and your buddies all around you. You work in a dot-com? I rest my case.

BULL'S HEAD TAVERN
295 3rd Ave. (22nd & 23rd Sts.)
Gramercy 212.685.2589

Twenty- and thirtysomething locals jam up three-deep at the bar in this otherwise quiet neighborhood. The daily happy hour runs from 1pm-7pm, and you can get 20 different draft varieties for $3 (Stella, Guinness, Harp are all in the lineup), as well as $3 frozen regular and strawberry margaritas. The Jim Roberti Band—performing a mix of original music and classic covers—comes in Thursday nights; on other nights, the pool tables, dart games, and Golden Tee electronic golf will keep you occupied.

CALIENTE CAB CO.
21 Waverly Pl. (@ Greene St.)
Greenwich Village 212.529.1500

61 7th Ave. South (@ Bleecker St.)
West Village 212.243.8517

A Tex-Mex joint with a weakness for American food—burgers and wings join burritos and quesadillas in a fun, veejayed environment. Salsa and hip-hop proliferate at the Waverly location, where you can expect discounted drinks daily from noon-8pm (Sunday-Thursday, the fun lasts an hour later). Margaritas are down to $4, well drinks are $3, and large frozen drinks are $8.50 (normally $13). Thursdays, the managers at Waverly Place throw a special themed party (they get creative; there's something called the tequila music award), with $2 beers and tequila shots and $4 margaritas.

CHERRY TAVERN
441 E. 6th St. (1st Ave. & Ave. A)
East Village 212.777.1448

A dive with personality, the Cherry Tavern has a local follow-ing so strong you can expect to stand. It's hot and crowded, but filled with some of the most interesting and fashionable people this side of 5th Avenue. Attitude? Sure, but if you can hack off your brand-new mullet and don a cool vintage tee it won't be a problem. The jukebox is known to have the most eclectic and amusing selections around and the pool table never sits idle. You can get a Rheingold & a shot for the infla-tion-free $5. As an added bonus, cans of Pabst Blue Ribbon are available in abundance for an unmentionably good price.

CUCINA ITALIANA PAPRIKA
110 St. Marks Pl. (1st & 2nd Aves.)
East Village 212.677.6563

Featuring a wonderful fusion of Northern Italian and Swiss cuisine, Paprika effectively prepares high-end food at prices that accommodate East Village bohemia (4pm-7pm prix fixe, $12.95). One semi-spacious, but well laid-out room with a thoughtful, minimalist décor combines subtle Italian village nuances with understated East Village charm. A warm staff promptly attends to small wooden tables, while a small bar that serves primarily to facilitate the seated diners offers an almost foolishly inexpensive wine list that includes a fantastic 2001 Badia al Monte Chianti ($24 for a bottle).

DOC HOLLIDAY'S
141 Ave. A (@ 9th St.)
East Village 212.979.0312

Doc Holliday's is a dive that makes the whole East Village experience worthwhile. The décor looks like Hunter S. Thompson went nuts in a Stetson shop. Doc's is often full of NYU kids coming in for the outrageous drink deals on Monday ($5 for ladies all-you-can-drink Bud and mixed drinks) and Tuesday ($7 for all-you-can-drink Bud Light) nights or the expected leather-and-denim East Village locals. These guys may look tough but they drink quietly and tell wonderful stories about the neighborhood if you've got the sack to ask them. This place can get a little crazy, but if you're thunder-drunk, it will all seem completely normal.

DOUBLE HAPPINESS
173 Mott St. (@ Broome St.)
NoLita 212.941.1282

Elegantly hip, Double Happiness has a magnetism rarely found in this day and age. A heart-stopping DJ spins the latest to keep the young, fashionable downtown crowd on its toes, be it in the main room swaying to the tunes or cuddling in the coveted nook at the end of the bar. Abacuses, small individually lit photographs above the honeycomb-tile floor, and crimson banquettes add a touch of mystery. Artists, musicians, slackers, and hackers all mingle in here late at night and get into the kind of trouble legends are made of. Fall in love or fall on the floor, anything goes. But the best part? The two-for-one happy hour, 6pm-7:30pm every night.

DOWN THE HATCH
179 W. 4th St. (6th & 7th Aves.)
West Village 212.627.9747

Isn't college over yet? If this bar were a Greek word, it would be fratus majorius. The equation remains the same: Many frat boys equals cheap beer, great wings, all sports all the time, and a no-holds-barred "drink 'til you drop" attitude, keeping this West Village hole in the wall a favorite for twelve years running. The weekend deal is the best: Doors open at noon Saturdays and Sundays for a five-hour, all-you-can-eat wings binge (official start is at 1pm). For $18, you get the wings and 12 drink tickets, which you can redeem for domestic pitchers (four tickets) or drafts (normally $3.50; here one ticket). Come weekdays, a 4pm-7pm happy hour means half-price drinks, including everything but premium stuff like martinis and Long Island Iced Tea. At 7pm, the fun cuts a different groove: Mondays outside of football season, it's $2 domestic bottles, Tuesdays bring $1 domestic drafts, Wednesdays (ladies' night) are $2 Jell-o shots and $3 Sam Adams Lights, Thursdays are $11 buckets of beer (five 12-oz. bottles) and $3 shots of kamikazes, house tequilas, and whatever else you did in college, and Sundays bring $2 drafts, including Sam Adams, Stella, and Hardcore Cider. Foosball is a major draw; regular tournaments draw a crowd. Will I feel like it's rush week? Yes. Will I want to tattoo a Greek letter on my ass by night's end? Yes. Will I fit in at a *Vogue* party after an hour in this bar? No fuckin' way.

FINNERTY'S
108 3rd Ave. (13th & 14th Sts.)
East Village 212.777.3363

"So what's your major? No kidding! That's mine too; you wanna throw some darts with me? Maybe go back to my place for some rub and tug?" You'll hear this conversation at least twice an hour at this haven for NYU students who will forego ambiance for a domestic and that new freshman honey from Mobile, Alabama. The good thing about Finnerty's is that you don't have to spend a lot to enjoy yourself. There's no happy hour; drinks are cheap from the moment the bar throws open its doors (11:30am). There are nightly shot specials at $2; Bud, Bud Light, and Red Wolf are $2 a pint and $7 a pitcher; and a generic well drink in a pint glass is only $6 (just $1 more for top-shelf). The scene doesn't get busy 'til around midnight—stupid homework.

THE GIN MILL
442 Amsterdam Ave. (81st & 82nd Sts.)
Upper West Side 212.580.9080

Bring us your poor, thirsty, hungry, and tired, searching for pool, foosball, Golden Tee, Pac-man, Megatouch, or a place to be a couch potato. The Gin Mill caters to all. The philosophy here is everything for everyone and they mean it. Come for happy hour (Monday-Friday, 4pm-8pm) or Ladies' Night and live it up old-school style with half-price drinks. Pick from DJs Thursday through Saturday or live music on Thursdays. Two large-screen televisions and 11 smaller ones keep the wallflowers occupied while a downstairs room provides a more intimate setting for the adventurous. Feel a bit farklempt? Take in some fresh air at the outdoor café—truly, they've got everything but a doctor's note for the next day. During the summer, those looking for hard bodies should stop In after work to check out the softball teams that come to rejuvenate after a hard game.

JAKE'S DILEMMA
430 Amsterdam Ave. (80th & 81st Sts.)
Upper West Side 212.580.0556

A bar this size looks mighty small when packed with twentysomethings over the moon about the drink specials. We know, it's not often a daily happy hour comes along. Here, it's half-price drinks Monday-Thursday 4pm-8pm, Friday 3pm-8pm, and Saturday and Sunday noon-7pm. Included are the 14 different draft beers; the champions among them: Sam Adams and Stella Artois. Also included are—read our lips—liquor and cocktails (ergo, all alcohol); it's possible to score a cosmopolitan, even if you're not scoring anything else, for the remarkable $3.50.

JEREMY'S ALE HOUSE
228 Front St. (Peck Slip & Beekman St.)
Financial District 212.964.3537

This is the Hogs & Heifers of the Financial District: a working-class bar with bras dancing on the walls. Lest they take anything away from the bar's solid, blue-collar machismo, Jeremy's—which serves Coors in 32-oz. mugs—showcases FDNY paraphernalia right alongside. But the weekday happy hour is the strangest thing: It's early (8am-10am), when most bartenders are still snoozing and the club kids are piling bleary-eyed out onto the street. Jeremy's is buzzing on Thursdays and Fridays with a hodge-podge of fish market workers, policemen, and firemen, all of whom want that 32-oz. beer for a measly $1.75. Everything else from the fully stocked bar is half-price.

LUDLOW BAR
165 Ludlow St. (Houston &
Stanton Sts.)
Lower East Side 212.353.0536

More club than bar, Ludlow's DJs tend to put their spin on house music, hip-hop, and anything else with a computer-generated beat. The music is far too loud for any real conversation, so don't plan on having one. Instead, come get your $3 beers and $4 cocktails from 6pm-9pm most nights (call first). If you want to dance, you've found nirvana. If not, then shimmy over to the pool table—a bit out of place here, but useful nonetheless.

MacDougal St. Ale House
122 MacDougal St. (Bleecker & W. 3rd Sts.)
Greenwich Village 212.254.8569

Pabst on tap. Pool table. Dartboard. Metallica tunes. It's pretty simple at MacDougal St. Ale House, and that's the way they like it. The happy hour draws the frat pack ($3 bottles of Heineken, Corona, and Amstel Light and $3 well drinks all day Monday and Tuesday, and $1 off the 12 drafts on Wednesday). The private and spacious dart room in the back makes a great place to get away from the occasionally raucous Saturday night meat market. Keep in mind that they take their darts as seriously as a heart attack in here, so don't go back there and think about chugging and chucking or you might wind up tacked to the wall for target practice. During the week, it's a great space to sit back and enjoy the whirring fans and the creature comforts of a big bar and a beer.

McSorley's Old Ale House
15 E. 7th St. (2nd & 3rd Aves.)
East Village 212.473.9148

You haven't been drunk in New York City until you've drunk yourself green at McSorley's. A classic Irish bar that has been a city fixture for more than 150 years, it gathers a mixture of young and old, hip and hip-replaced, but everybody in here is always having a good time. Beware of McSorley's on St. Paddy's Day! This is the place where out-of-towners come all decked out in green and ready to drink until they puke and if you happen to be in the way, not even the luck of the Irish can help you. In addition to $2 beers (or two for $3.50), McSorley's serves a mean burger and mashed potatoes, which tend to get overlooked by some of the more medicated patrons. If you can't have a good time in here, you must be dead.

NEVADA SMITH'S
74 3rd Ave. (11th & 12th Sts.)
East Village 212.982.2591

GOOOAL!! Yes, this is soccer, ahem, football headquarters, so if you're into the slow-paced sport with the funny checkered ball, this is the spot for you. When the big matches are on, time zones be damned! These early risers pack the joint at ungodly hours to get all liquored up and noisy. It's an experience like no other and for us Americans weaned on Monday Night Football and professional wrestling, we can appreciate the raw, unbridled enthusiasm Nevada's patrons possess. However, on the days and nights it doesn't have football matches it turns into your run-of-the mill, predictable NYU frat hangout. If that's for you, drop in weekdays from 11am-midnight for $2 Bud drafts and $2 shots of kamikaze and purple hooters.

NO IDEA
30 E. 20th St. (Broadway & Park Ave. South)
Gramercy 212.777.0100

What'd you do last night? No idea. The name says it all. Popular with area suits and students of the NY Film Academy, you can feel the love in this part sports bar, part singles scene. Happy hour packs the cheery crowd in for pool and that all-important pastime, drinking yourself stupid. The "hour" starts at 4pm and runs all night; come in for $5 pint-sized house mixed drinks (vodka cranberry is on the list, cosmopolitans are not). If your name matches their "name of the day," you'll get free draft beers or house mixed drinks from 5pm-11pm. Oh, yeah!

OFF THE WAGON
109 MacDougal St. (W. 3rd & Bleecker Sts.)
Greenwich Village 212.533.4487

If you're looking for a lawyer, look no further than this sporty, all-American spot. Attorneys-to-be abound at this major NYU Law School hangout, but you don't have to be studying for the Bar to enjoy this bar. Despite generic, Alpha Beta Crappa features like huge plastic beer bargain banners, the space is truly singular. The two-story bar full of rich, polished wood is also full of authentic city energy left over from the days when the building housed the Derby Steak House—a former neighborhood staple. Amuse yourself with the easygoing bartenders, inexpensive brews, and flirty chicks or indulge in OTW's myriad of distractions, from pool to addictive video games to darts. Should you fall off the wagon, this is one hell of a place to land. And it may be your only chance to beat the hell out of a lawyer!

RESERVOIR BAR & GRILL
70 University Pl. (10th & 11th Sts.)
Greenwich Village 212.475.0770

Walking the fine line between academics and alcoholism, this post-frat hang-out offers $3 pints, heavy food, and plenty of sports to the baseball cap-wearing masses that stroll University Place in search of their long-lost college days, or the college days they are currently squandering. Irish pub meets sports bar meets roadhouse in this straight-up watering hole which features a pool table and a Golden Tee video game tournament for the would-be-athlete who enjoys any sport that doesn't involve his needing to leave the bar stool. Ladies, feel free to visit—they'll be happy to see you. Mr. Right is probably not here, but Mr. Right Now might be willing to buy you a drink or six.

RODEO BAR
375 3rd Ave. (26th & 27th Sts.)
Gramercy 212.683.6500

Got a hankerin' for down-home hillbilly fun? Look no further than Rodeo Bar! With live music seven nights a week and not a cover charge in sight, house favorites like Earl Pickens and the Black Mountain Marauders treat the packed room to a dang good time and will surely two-step their way deep into your heart. With award-winning margaritas served from a bona fide horse-trailer-turned-bar, fiery Tex-Mex fare, and free peanuts on every table, it's no wonder Rodeo Bar remains New York's premiere Southern road-house and longest-running honky-tonk.

RUDY'S BAR AND GRILL
627 9th Ave. (44th & 45th Sts.)
Hell's Kitchen 212.974.9169

Cozy in a cramped sort of way, Rudy's well-worn interior is bathed in dim, warm lighting from a row of imitation Tiffany lamps over the bar. The long space features a wall of round, cushioned booths where the young and noisy take up residence and don't move for hours. Rudy's has the cheapest drinks in town, including a serviceable selection of $3 drafts (Bud) and $3.25 well drinks. Most importantly, Rudy's offers free hot dogs to anyone who wants them. They are only given out intermittently, however, so if you want one, you gotta stay on your toes.

SOPHIE'S
509 E. 5th St. (Aves. A & B)
East Village 212.228.5680

There's no sign outside, and once you walk in, you know that wasn't an oversight. The dive bar's business comes by word of mouth, so the crowd inside needs no introductions. Sophie's is the rendezvous point for all of the city's bike messengers (witness: tree at the entrance, chained to suffocation). Why not— $2 McSorley's are hard to come by. The drinks are cheap, the pool is fair, and the bar's a bar. What a relief.

SUEDE
161 W. 23rd St. (6th & 7th Aves.)
Chelsea 212.633.6113

Chocolate martinis, a well-designed space, great music, and a place to dance…what do these have in common? No, it's not Rupert Everett's living room, it's Suede. The loft-like space is 3,200 square feet, with two bars on two levels, a rare cabaret license, and a good-looking young crowd. Try the tasty signature drinks: the Flirtini and the Suede Martini.

SWIFT HIBERNIAN LOUNGE
34 E. 4th St. (Broadway & Lafayette St.)
NoHo 212.227.9438

Named after Jonathan Swift, the Swift Lounge—sister bar to nearby Puck Fair—is a rustic little pub reminiscent of the Irish homestead, replete with church pews for booths and a worn pulpit. Nab a seat in either room—there are lots of nooks and crannies to wile away the hours. Swift serves a good selection of a few dozen beers on tap, including some of Ireland's greatest hits: Harp, Bass, Fullers, and Boddingtons. Belgian beers and American microbrews also figure into the equation. But best of all is this: a 20oz. Guinness for all of $5.

TORTILLA FLATS
767 Washington St. (@ W. 12th St.)
West Village 212.243.1053

This rollicking West Village bar would be a prime spot for a hoedown if it had hay. It doesn't. But the hay-less Mexican restaurant/bar, best known for overstuffed burritos and Monday and Tuesday bingo nights, does have a Monday-Friday happy hour from 4pm-7pm (and 1pm-4am on Saturdays) serving two-for-one Rolling Rocks and $5.00 off margarita pitchers.

AQUAGRILL
210 Spring St. (@ 6th Ave.)
SoHo 212.274.0505

The "Closed" sign on Aquagrill should say, "Gone fishin'" because the fish are so fresh here they're still flopping. And that includes the raw bar up front that will have you doing a little happy dance in no time. Oysters and white wine in an energetic and airy atmosphere—could there be a better date place? The outdoor seating in good weather is coveted real estate, second only to the Hamptons and much easier to bear. Bring a date or a friend from out of town and spend the afternoon impressing them with the excellent people-watching and easy breezes inside and out. Best of all, on Tuesday-Friday from 4pm-6pm, blue point oysters are only $1.

BB DOYLE'S
302 W. 51st St. (@ 8th Ave.)
Hell's Kitchen 212.541.7080

You've got to love a good old Irish pub that doesn't mind serving Anheuser-Busch's version of Guinness (Bare Knuckle Stout). There are good drink deals here to match the laid-back ambiance: Beers of the month—such as Brooklyn Lager—are $3.50 per pint. But mostly, I'm sending you here for the food: During cold weather (about October-April), the pub puts out some type of hot dish from 5pm-7pm. We're talking hearty British fare à la beef stew or shepherd's pie for those old winter mornings.

CALICO JACK'S
800 2nd Ave. (42nd & 43rd Sts.)
Midtown 212.557.4300

You can hear Calico Jack's before you see it, overflowing every evening with weaving baseball caps and the teetering mini-dresses that follow them. You won't be leaving hungry, thirsty, or sober, as drafts go for $2-$3 until 4:30pm. There is karaoke every Tuesday at 10pm and a Manhattan Beach Party every summer Saturday offering $3 Coronas and mixed drinks to go with the DJ spinning '80s, hip-hop, reggae, and house music. Best of all, Thursdays from 5pm-7pm bring a Mexican buffet (think tacos and fried jalapenos) and all you can-drink anything, all for a 10-spot. Fun and rambunctious, Calico Jack's will erase your memory one shot at a time.

CUCINA DI PESCE
87 E. 4th St. (2nd & 3rd Aves.)
East Village 212.260.6800

Don't question, just do. From 4pm to closing, this bar and restaurant gives away free mussels to inspire its young patrons to, well, come in and eat mussels. The staff is emphatic: Don't buy anything, just sit here and enjoy the mussels…aren't they wonderful? We shucked them this morning…leaving a more discriminating, less hungry person to guess at the motivations (mussel surplus?). Still, I've never known anyone to get sick, and the alternating, steamed preparations—with marinara sauce, or garlic, white wine, and onions—are quite palatable, even good, whether you get them at the bar, in the restaurant, the garden, or the romantic hearth room. You might come to freeload, but it's almost inevitable you won't (with the staff being so nice, and all). Right?

FIVE POINTS
31 Great Jones St. (@ Lafayette St.)
NoHo 212.253.5700

This elegant bar/restaurant in this distinctly non-elegant neighborhood attracts an odd mix of bankers, fashionistas, and artists young and old. The mix becomes odder still during the unbelievable happy hour. The deal: $1 oysters and $5 martinis. The catch: finding yourself a spot. Get there good and early; the bar is short and the tables few. If your harried bartender does what ours did, and hands you a dozen of the slimy suckers for the price of a half, then it would not be the time to skimp on tips.

MIRCHI'S
29 7th Ave. South (Bedford & Morton Sts.)
West Village 212.414.0931

The tawas—round cast-iron griddles mounted over an open fire—are the main attraction at this contemporary Indian restaurant. Cooking street food appetizers over them with metal spatulas creates a characteristic "tuk tuk" sound which resonates throughout the restaurant. But what really brings in the crowds to this minimalist Indian bistro is the 3pm-8pm

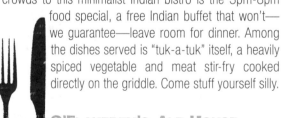

food special, a free Indian buffet that won't—we guarantee—leave room for dinner. Among the dishes served is "tuk-a-tuk" itself, a heavily spiced vegetable and meat stir-fry cooked directly on the griddle. Come stuff yourself silly.

O'FLAHERTY'S ALE HOUSE
334 W. 46th St. (8th & 9th Aves.)
Hell's Kitchen 212.581.9366

O'Flaherty's Ale House, in Hell's Kitchen since the 1920s, has the kind of character that comes—if at all—with age and experience. This Irish pub's winding bar offers a selection of drinks and beers at working-man's prices (pints $4.50; mixed drinks $5) and has heard a few tales you wouldn't repeat to your mother. The Irish pub is brightly lit to highlight the intellectual décor: paintings, book-shelves, a fireplace, and—who are we kidding?—a pool table and dartboard. At 10pm, the bar staff puts out a free dish, usually something hearty like meat ziti. At 10:30pm, the live music begins, but don't worry, it won't interfere with your plans to take over the world. When the weather's nice, the outdoor garden area is open until 10:30pm.

PRAVDA
281 Lafayette St. (Prince & Houston Sts.)
SoHo 212.226.4696

Now that the Cold War is ancient history and communism is cool, Pravda is cashing in. The elegant vodka/caviar bar is famous for its model clientele and house-infused martinis (in that order), but don't worry, at $11-$13 for a long stem of liquid seduction, I wouldn't send you there for the cheap drinks. The first hour of every night, waiters bring out free platters of the food du mois. Here's hoping that the bar brings back the free Zakouski ("small foods" in Russian) platter— 12 bite-sized appetizers served on a wooden tray (now $19). In the meantime, enjoy treats that are no less good but slightly more economical, such as homemade potato chips stained with beet juice and served alongside a crème fraiche caviar dip.

Once you get behind the velvet rope (a feat in itself sometimes), door charges at NYC dance clubs are often $20 and up. But if you're paying those prices, you're not keeping your eyes wide open. Practically every club in NYC makes postcards available to frequent customers, offering $5+ discounts off of cover charges; party promoters—who are in the volume business by nature—are rich sources of discounts, too.

BAIRD JONES HOTLINE
212.340.1233

Baird isn't a clothing label, nor is he a rock star: He's one of the city's most successful party promoters, and he has a nice-guy attitude to boot. The man has an answering machine with a mile-long capacity for greetings, and he uses it to direct the nightlife of happy-go-lucky subscribers the city over. The daily 411 for an entire week of club and bar parties is delivered in an affable enthusiast's voice whose owner goes into the nitty gritty: whether boys have to wear collared shirts, what time the line gets long, how to recognize the friendly bouncer, how to deal with parking (indicating a Bridge and Tunnel vibe), and most importantly…when the hours are for open bar, and what the magic pass phrase is for free admission. That saves you $20+ off of a cover charge. If it's your birthday and you run into Jones (he tells you how to find him), he'll buy you a bottle of champagne. NYU-proximate Webster Hall figures highly on Jones' list, as do Lot 61, Discotheque, China Club, and NV.

BAR 169
169 E. Broadway (@ Rutgers St.)
Lower East Side 212.473.8866

In a nearly bar-free pocket of Chinatown, this spacious exception half a story below East Broadway draws cool kids from all over the city minus the cooler-than-thou crap that usually comes along with them. The simple room is lined with diner-style pleather booths and TVs that hang over either end of the magnificently long bar. If you need to pass some time before it's your turn at Ms. Pac-Man, you can always shoot some pool or one-up your buddies at one of the trivia machines. Weekends bring name-brand DJs (DJ Alex, Champion Soul, Swing Set) spinning house and hip-hop; the cover charge is never over $5. One unusual point of interest: You'll be surprised to find that they serve everything from burgers to spring rolls, and it's all delicious.

CAFÉ WHA
115 MacDougal St. (W. 3rd & Bleecker Sts.)
Greenwich Village 212.254.3706

You can't dance in the aisles here, mostly because there's little in the way of space. These days, the legendary below-ground rock club is home to a very good house band that plays danceable covers—with no cover if you get there before 10:45pm. That happens Wednesdays and Fridays; on all other days, there's a resident Brazilian ensemble, a vintage funk/comedy show, reggae music, and various other special events. The place fills up fast, so unless you reserve your tickets in advance ($5, $10, or $12, depending on the day and the event), you might find yourself blowing all your savings on a little something extra for the bouncer.

CODA
34 E. 34th St. (@ Madison Ave.)
Midtown 212.685.3434

Don't let the ol' velvet rope/bouncer routine keep you away from this live music lounge. Coda doesn't have that snobbish attitude you'd expect from a swanky spot with a Murray Hill address. At first glance, you'd never know a bank once occupied this large, high-ceilinged space, but venture downstairs to "the vault" and you're sure to be clued in—the safety deposit boxes lining the wall of the retro-furnished loft inspire naughty make-out fantasies. Weekdays are for live bands, but weekends are for DJs. When you're tired, slip onto a cushy cranberry couch and nibble on trendy appetizers like the brie, Roquefort, and wild mushroom fondue or Southwestern spring rolls. Wash it all down with one of Coda's sweet drink concoctions like Whole Lotta Love or Tush (try ordering that one without blushing). Cool music, cool crowd—sounds like some good reasons to get in tune with Coda.

P.S.1 CONTEMPORARY ART CENTER
22–25 Jackson Ave. (@ 46th Ave.)
Long Island City 718.784.2084

Warm Up parties—drawing crowds in excess of 5,000 happy folks—happen every Saturday from the first weekend in July to Labor Day. Tickets are only $6, and the party is a huge fundraiser for the museum despite the inexpensive cover. Beers are $3.50 and food—catered by the museum's own café—consists of sandwiches and other offerings. In the courtyard—and here's the clincher—dancers are enclosed in the winning installation for the annual Young Architects' Program, co-sponsored by nearby MoMA. Past DJs have included Richie Houghton, Nicky Siano, The Mad Professor, and Africa Bambaataa. P.S.1's estimable galleries—ordinarily entered with a suggested donation of $5—are open throughout.

SAPPHIRE LOUNGE
249 Eldridge St. (Houston & Stanton Sts.)
Lower East Side 212.777.5153

Oh no, I didn't! Oh yes, you did shake your ass like that at Sapphire Lounge. This venerable mini-disco lures fun seekers with DJs blasting the best of Hot 97, a low cover charge ($5), and an attitude-free vibe. The crowd is a mix of hip-hop enthusiasts, a rare breed of inoffensive Bridge and Tunnel types, and curious local hipsters, and they're all grinding away on the intimate dance floor having way too much fun to notice the somewhat tacky surroundings. Scene-seekers and wallflowers should go elsewhere, but if you're in the mood to bust a move without sleazy come-ons, Sapphire is priceless.

SIX6SEVEN BAR GALLERY LOUNGE
667 Fulton St. (Ashland Pl. & Rockwell Pl.)
Fort Greene 718.855.8558

This place wants to be a stylish den for denizens of the urban underground and takes a crack at it with an ostensibly impressive corner of velvet rope outside its door, nearly pitch-black interior with pulsating, loud underground house (Saturdays and Wednesdays), and a swank back room with yet another roped-off velvet leopard-print VIP booth. But Six6Seven also desires to be desired by those in the market for a friendly and fun after-work refuge. To this end, there are three TVs, which—besides a disco ball circulating the light of a dozen candles and red lamps—are the primary source of light inside. Fun for everyone, gay nights are on Sundays, karaoke on Tuesdays, and hip-hop/R&B on Tuesdays and Fridays. Very dark and very loud, in order to enjoy it your modus operandi should be to dance, not to talk. On the dance floor here, existential questions take a back seat to lounge areas where the predators can track their prey before pouncing to the beats.

Being a dedicated sports fan in NYC comes with its penalties, starting not least with the steep prices for spectator tickets during the occasional trip to the stadium. Well, you can get the same ballpark ambiance in stadiums that play host to major league soccer and minor league and university teams—and still have money for beer and dogs.

BROOKLYN CYCLONES
KeySpan Park
1904 Surf Ave. (@ W. 17th St.)
Coney Island 718.449.8497

In spring 2003, American baseball fans flocked to the fields in record-breaking numbers...to watch minor league ball games. It was a frigid spring, so blame it on the economy, or just reap the benefits. To see the young Brooklyn Cyclones, non-obstructed outfield bleacher seats are only $5, field box seats don't top $11, and season tickets (all in the infield) range from $266-$418. The official farm team for the Mets, the Cyclones share an owner and the occasional player with the major leaguers (Mets relief pitcher Mike Stanton made a rehab start here). But the real fun is in the setting: The right field wall of the stadium is just 50 feet from the Coney Island boardwalk. No need to choose: You can have a clear view of the field, the Atlantic, and the tall twinkling Ferris wheel. Don't underestimate these owners; they know how to stoke your wheel of fun, throwing in Friday night fireworks and plenty of silly between-inning activities, such as a mustard racing against a ketchup and a relish, sponsored by nearby

Nathan's…all the better to go with your $3.50 dog. Note: For group fun, luxury boxes—which hold 18 people—run $1,000-$1,500, and the Ocean View Party Deck lets up to 75 of your closest friends see all of Coney Island for $2,500. The box office told me to tell you that tickets are always available on game day.

NY/NJ METROSTARS
Giants Stadium
50 Route 120
Secaucus 201.583.7000

Everyone agrees that soccer in America doesn't get the attention it deserves. Well, a revolution has got to start somewhere, and why not New Jersey? The major league MetroStars—red-and-black-striped players representing the entire metropolitan area—deserve some of your attention, having won more than half their scheduled games in the early part of 2003. The season—and all 17 home games—takes place mid April to mid October. If you love the sound of a "goooooooooooal," part-season tickets (seven games) will run you $136-$280. On game day, bleacher seats range from $18-$38.

THE RED STORM
St. John's University
Belson Stadium
8000 Utopia Pkwy. (@ Union Tpke.)
Jamaica 718.990.2000

As if you didn't have reason enough to go to Jamaica, Queens, try this brand-new stadium where you can watch the six-time Big East Tournament Champions elude another challenger running around the all-grass field. The Red Storm boast one of the country's elite college soccer programs and in recent years have consistently been ranked in the top 10 in the national polls. Tickets are typically less than $10, even during playoffs.

STATEN ISLAND YANKEES
Richmond County Bank Ballpark
75 Richmond Terrace (@ Wall St.)
Staten Island 718.720.9265

More imperfect? Sure. More fascinating for their flaws? You bet. For plenty of New Yorkers, the S.I. Yanks—frequent NY-Penn League champions—are the better Yankees. It'll never cost more than $10 (versus $80) for a box seat in a stadium 1/6 the size. There's no endless climbing, no pushy crowds, no shitty views. With 38 home games, plus best-of-three divisional playoffs (here's hoping)—you do the math; season tickets are only $380, with a free night of practice and preferred seating for stadium music events thrown in for good measure. So the season—mid-June to early September—is a little shorter than the majors, which is probably just as well. Even going "all out" entails—at top end—all of $2,750 for the Skyline Suite, an air-conditioned party room that holds 60 people and features a kitchen, bar, tables, leather sofas, Direct TV system (should you care to watch something else), scorecards, free popcorn and sodas, and outdoor seating. As with the arena in the Bronx, don't bring any outside food (hot dogs are $2.50).

U.S. OPEN QUALIFYING TOURNAMENT
USTA National Tennis Center (@ Grand Central Pkwy. West) Flushing Meadows, Queens
www.usopen.org

The world's richest tennis tournament—with a kitty upwards of $17 million—is also the most watched. But paying top dollar to see the Annas and Andres compete—as exciting as that is—is also highly unoriginal, especially when you can be there to witness first-hand the birth of a star—for free. The week before the Open kicks off has four days of nail-biting qualifying matches, which determine which of the up-and-coming players will make it into the main draw. If you can't get the weekdays off, join in the fun with a weekend's worth of practice events—also free, free, free.

Not every New Yorker chalks off his game time to the Times' easy Monday crossword. Here are some ideas for broadening the horizons.

BOWLMOR LANES
110 University Pl. (12th & 13th Sts.)
Greenwich Village 212.255.8188

Being a bowler in NYC has a different connotation than elsewhere. If you bowl in suburbia, you might not think twice about scooping a wedgie out of your crack before lining up your shot. But if you bowl in the city, heaven knows that fashion is more important than knocking down a few stupid pins. Bowling owes its cool urban image to this elevated, ultramodern bar/lounge, which has been around since 1938. Get one glimpse of the stainless steel lobby and the polished neon surfaces, and you'd shudder to use the word "alley." Ordinarily, the $6.45-$8.95 per person charge per game ($5 for shoe rental) could make you scuttle out of there faster than your latest gutter ball (hey, no one ever said cool bowlers were good). But on Monday nights starting at 10pm, it's a city bowler's chance to get better. Night Strikes—unlimited bowling for $20 a person—gives you the bowling ball your dad never knew: The lights go out, blacklights come up, the pins become glow-in-the-dark, and live DJs come in, keeping the place in techno and house until the wee hours (3am). Of course there's a bar. School night? Like it'd even occur to you to play by those rules.

LUNCH-HOUR BACKGAMMON & CHESS
Upper Room Battery Park City (Albany St. & Hudson River) Battery Park City
212.528.2733

It's more like a lunch hour and a half, but here's somewhere you can play worthy opponents for free.

PETE'S CANDY STORE
709 Lorimer St. (Richardson & Frost Sts.) Williamsburg
718.302.3770

On select nights, this rockin' venue (see Rock Cheap) doubles as a game parlor for quiz night, Scrabble, and a newfangled knitting thing called Stitch 'n Bitch. Guys, keep an open mind—your metrosexualized peers are darning socks by the dozen. Call ahead for times.

TORTILLA FLATS
767 Washington St. (@ W. 12th St.) West Village 212.243.1053

This popular Mexican tostada joint is game central all through the week, host to free Monday and Tuesday bingo nights, Wednesday hula-hooping contests, and Sunday trivia nights. Be a champ and take home a bottle of hot sauce. Other funness abounds, including a strange obsession with 1960s actor Ernest Borgnine (*McHale's Navy*), which says nothing about the patron age range.

Our skyscraper forest is hardly devoid of green spaces. Leaving aside the obvious parks, recreational spaces—replete with green paths, waterways, and lush gardens—abound.

BRONX ZOO
2300 Southern Blvd. (Garden & E. 182nd Sts.)
Bronx 718.220.5100

In the great zoo debate, there are the traditionalists who still swear by this Bronx standby. With over 265 acres, 4,000 animals, and creative exhibits like Tiger Mountain and JungleWorld, an indoor rainforest, this flagship of zoos—which opened in 1899—still makes for a terrific day's outing 365 days a year. On Wednesdays, when the regular adult ticket ($11) becomes a suggested entry fee, the day becomes a bargain. Another deal: If it's rainy or getting there, grab the nearest kid and get him/her in for free. (Call the hotline to confirm.) For all you animal rightists: Chill, the zoo is linked to wildlife conservation, which means that if you can bring yourself to shell out the extra $3 for the Congo Gorilla Forest, you can elect for the money to go to conservation efforts in Africa.

TIPS FOR ZOOING SMART

The clever people that designed the zoo's website have enabled you to plan your trip from the online map. Check out the links to "must see" areas, and vivid descriptions of all the rest. They also suggest you go in winter, when you'll encounter fewer crowds and get to see the truly beautiful holiday light display—one of the city's best traditions. And if you can't get Wednesdays off, the zoo often partners with businesses that dole out money-saving coupons. Transportation note: It costs $7 to park your car, $8 to take the Liberty Lines express bus round-trip, and $2 to use your MTA card in the subway, one way, with many stops from Manhattan. Choose your poison.

BROOKLYN BOTANIC GARDEN
1000 Washington Ave. (@ Montgomery St.)
Prospect Heights 718.623.7200

Hugging the edge of Prospect Park near the Brooklyn Museum is a patch of dirt that Brookynites would love to keep to themselves. With 52 acres of trees, ponds, paths, and flowers, their very own Botanic Garden provides the kind of manicured respite that can satisfy a wide variety of tastes—and moods. Want to smell some roses? Gaze into a Japanese reflecting pool? Sit on a wooden bench near an English garden cottage? Listen to frogs in a lily pond? It's all here. The $5 admission fee is waived on Tuesdays and Saturday mornings (from 10am-12pm), on winter weekdays, and for members.

CENTRAL PARK WILDLIFE CENTER AND TISCH CHILDREN'S ZOO
East entrance (63rd & 66th Sts.)
Central Park 212.439.6500

The good news is that a Bronx trek isn't necessary to see decent wildlife. Although not as big, the Central Park Wildlife Center can quench your animal fix for less than you'd pay for a cosmopolitan and a good bit healthier ($3.50 for adults, $1.50 for seniors, and free for children under two). See the giant

polar bear doing the back-
stroke! See the colorful
birds in the Enchanted
Forest! See the sea lions frol-
icking in their glass-sided pool!
Within the center, the Tisch
Children's Zoo is technically
for the stroller set, but that's
no reason the bigger kids
can't get a peek and a giggle too at the snort-
ing potbelly pig and other so-called "domestic" animals. This is admittedly a kid-friendly zoo: On the hour, the
big clock at the entrance to the children's zoo plays a nurs-
ery rhyme, accompanied by dancing, cymbal-crashing animals. Charmed? Can you help it?

THE CLOISTERS
Fort Tryon Park
Upper West Side 212.923.3700

Medieval Europe is the last thing you'd expect to find cling-
ing like so much fuzzy vine on the edge of The Hudson River,
but the Cloisters—so named after the quadrangle-like struc-
tures that take after medieval French monasteries—brings
you a little piece of the era courtesy of the Metropolitan
Museum of Art. You won't find any wine production here, but
you will find magnificent columns framing beautifully tended
gardens. When you're ready to go in, check out the wide collection of illuminated manuscripts, stained glass, and tapes-
tries in the main building's galleries.

CHARLES A. DANA DISCOVERY CENTER
110th St. (5th & Lenox Aves.)
Central Park 212.860.1370

The Discovery Center is the launching point for nature tours covering every square inch of Central Park. This includes bird-watching, a "Central Park Adirondacks" hike, garden tours, and fishing.

Catfish, bluegills, bass, and carp: All are to be had—if for mere moments. This is catch-and-release fishing, and it goes on from April to October at the edge of Central Park's ponds and rivers. For all you animal rightists out there, take it easy: Catching fish to let 'em slip back in isn't mean at all when you're using barb-less hooks. The Discovery Center provides everything you need except the canvas hat.

At year's end, don't miss the ritual lighting ceremony. Everyone there chips in and makes an ornament, then puts it on the slender fir tree. The tree gets lit, everyone applauds, and the band plays. It's a good time.

5 LIVE cheap

Now it's time to go back to the basics. In this chapter, we show you how to decorate your apartment (no milk crates allowed!), eat food that doesn't include ramen noodles, travel within and out of the city, entertain and impress your pals, and still have enough pocket money for a few CDs, DVDs, and books. After all, what's the point of living in this city if you're going to be subsisting on raisins and sleeping on the floor of your empty studio? Feeling lonely? Getting mar-

ried in NYC isn't as expensive as you think—this chapter offers tips on how to say "I Do" without going bankrupt. Prefer animals over people? Adopting a pet is a low-cost way to add some fun to your life—and helps animals in need. We'll also guide you through the city's most exciting festivals and parades, plus show you how to get Internet access for cheap. Get a life—without spending a fortune.

Outfitting an apartment stylishly can easily be the biggest expenditure in your life. Check out these spots to do the job on the cheap.

ABC CARPET AND HOME

1055 Bronx River Ave. (@ Bruckner Blvd.)
Bronx 718.842.8772

Tanger Outlet Center III
1947 Old Country Rd.
Riverhead 631.208.1720

The two-story Bronx outlet—which supplies its smaller, Riverhead sister—of the city's most admired furniture store covers an entire city block, with separate departments for linens, beds, rugs, and the biggie: furniture. It's rare to find a damaged or discontinued item here—an on-premises repair shop takes care of gluing broken chair legs and getting unsightly stains off of rugs. What is common is a $1,200 kid leather sofa: Most items·are either current or a few seasons old, except of course the one-of-a-kind antiques from places like East India and Pakistan. Hold onto your chairs—the hundreds of sofas, tables, rugs, etc. can sell for 10-80 percent less than their Flatiron counterparts. In the Bronx, the advantage to staying in the city is obvious: You won't have to wait much more than three or four days. Better make sure you really love that zebra sofa; everything here is a final sale.

DYNASTY SUPERMARKET
68 Elizabeth St. (@ Hester St.)
Chinatown 212.966.4943

In this giant Chinese food emporium lies a treasure trove of possibilities for your urbane Pottery Barn-esque apartment. Namely: the dish aisle. Find rows of ironware, pottery, and ceramics—lily-shaped sauce servers, elongated sushi platters, rice bowls edged with bamboo designs, chunky tea mugs picturing classical brush landscapes. Satisfy a whim, pick up a gift, do your whole dining room. Everything is crafted in some faraway place (Japan, China, Thailand) Nothing tops $12. So yes, you have to be fond of things Asian. But no, you don't have to serve sushi therein.

POTTERY BARN
Tanger Outlet Center III
1770 W. Main St.
Riverhead 631.369.7699

You'll feel like you've stepped through the pages of a catalog, and by golly, you have. More chaotic and less well lit, this discount outlet of the mass good-taste emporium stocks everything the full retail stores and glossy catalogs do, at 30% off retail prices. In addition to items from the current season, you'll stumble across the usual warehouse finds, discontinued and damaged items at even more of a discount. Come in and wander among velvet armchair and ottoman sets, monogrammed sheet sets, and whimsical lamps. After 30 days, any merchandise that doesn't move goes down another 20%. I found a country patchwork quilt, ordinarily $200, for $70. The only drawback is getting here and getting it home. If you're buying furniture and don't have access to a truck, you might want to hold off until you have to outfit the whole apartment: The added cost of shipping can easily obliterate your savings.

IKEA
1100 Broadway Mall
Hicksville, LI 516.681.4532

1000 IKEA Dr. (@ Elizabeth Ctr.)
Elizabeth, NJ 908.289.4488

The Scandinavian king of cheap, sturdy furniture needs no introduction. But not everyone knows about the free bus service to the Elizabeth store on weekends from Port Authority. Departures are on the half-hour; call 800.BUS.IKEA.

DUMPSTER DIVING

No, the phrase isn't pretty. Neither is the activity. You're unlikely to actually jump head-first into a dumpster, but if you see a scuffed red velvet armchair that would go perfectly with your flea market book-shelf...you're not going to leave it by the side of the road, are you? My first piece of advice is that good finds are always to be had in NYC—the sanitation department considers bulk collections fair game at every pick-up.

There is truly no city in the U.S. like NYC for good, inexpensive eats…particularly in the realm of ethnic food, where authentic entrées in filling portions consistently cost $5 or $8. And here's where the recession has brought another windfall: The trend in gourmet cafés and bistro-type restaurants is to serve inexpensive tapas-size portions of creative, ethnic-inflected dishes. I've listed a selection here.

NOTE: Carry a small wad of bills; some of these joints are cash only. Cheap eats can be found throughout Chinatown and the Mediterranean enclaves of Queens, but we have highlighted a few favorites.

AKA CAFÉ
49 Clinton St. (Rivington & Stanton Sts.)
Lower East Side 212.979.6096

The owners of this former clothing shop pulled a nifty hat trick when they transformed it convincingly into a Latin bistro. The place's days in fashion aren't entirely forgotten: The emphasis everywhere is on pretty. Get a load of the centerpiece on top of the bar, a fishbowl filled to the brim with Spanish chardonnay and brandy-marinated fruit. The menu includes both Sunday brunch, and the larger-than-tapas "hot plates," all for an average main course price of $10.50. The heavier the better: Think flaky, meat- or vegetable-stuffed empanadas and slider sandwiches bubbling with a delicious, garlicky pink "salsa rosada."

AU BON PAIN

Various locations throughout the five boroughs, including:

425 Lexington Ave. • 122 E. 42nd St. • 1251 6th Ave. • The Newscorp Building (1211 6th Ave.) • 22 W. 52nd St. • The Port Authority Bus Terminal (625 8th Ave.) • 444 Madison Ave. 600 Lexington Ave. • 16 E. 44th St. • 420 5th Ave. • Macy's Department Store (151 W. 34th St.) • 6 Union Sq. East • The World Financial Center (200 Liberty St.) • 60 Broad St. • 222 Broadway • 73 5th Ave. • 58 E. 8th St. • 600 3rd Ave. • 1 Metrotech Ctr. (Brooklyn)

One of the best NYC coffeeshop/bakeries has devised a scheme that benefits both buyer and seller. Seller has excess baked goods in the afternoon and wants to get rid of them, to start afresh. Buyer gets to swoop them up at a drastic cut-rate: 50% off regular price. So go between 4pm-6pm to stock up on fresh and tasty cookies, crumb cakes, breadsticks, bagels, and scones. What do you know? Just in time for afternoon tea.

BAHAR SHISHKEBAB HOUSE
984 Coney Island Ave. (@ Parkville Ave.)
Kensington 718.434.8088

82-19 Queens Blvd (@ 74th St.)
Elmhurst 718.426.5822

You never know, you might one day find yourself in the thick of Coney Island Avenue. And perhaps you'll make it a point to, because in addition to being cheap, this is probably the best kebab house in town—and the only Afghani restaurant in Brooklyn. If you're not familiar with Afghani food, think of it as Persian fused with Indian or Pakistani. The best thing here is the $4.95 bolani kadu, a thin, pan-fried pastry stuffed with a sweet pumpkin filling—great around Thanksgiving. Nothing tops $16, including juicy morgh (boneless chicken in a tangy marinade) and lamb tika kebabs, manto (meat-stuffed dumplings with tomato and minted yogurt sauce), kabli palow (basmati with stewed lamb and steamed carrots and raisins), and bangan burani (eggplant with garlic and herbs). Beware the rice—at worst it can be rubbery and dried out—but the chicken soup and salads are good. End with outstanding goshifeel (fried dough dribbled with honey and pistachios) and Afghani tea (with ground cardamom).

BISCUIT
367 Flatbush Ave. (7th Ave. & Sterling Pl.)
Park Slope 718.398.2227

At home or not, barbeque is the most sociable thing you can do with food, short of a food fight. But in a city where grills are as rare as Komodo dragons, rib joints like Biscuit can save the day. Biscuit is so home-grown that the smoking, curing, and biscuit-rolling are all done on the premises, the latter by a gourmet baker who used to turn out tarts for the rich and famous in TriBeCa. Everything comes on paper plates with extra handi-wipes. Come here for Mr. Brown, a white bun stuffed with barbequed pork shoulder ($6.50), pulled chicken ($6.50), or a catfish sandwich ($6.50). Add a side of mac and cheese for $3.25. What could be simpler, cheaper, or more rib-sticking?

Bus Stop Café
597 Hudson St. (@ Bethune St.)
West Village 212.206.1100

Pass up the Paris Commune across the street: Cute as it is, you'll be whisked out the door in no time without so much as a "Good-Day" for all the money you've blown on Sunday brunch. Diner food is served all day at this no-nonsense spot, and the bustling weekend vibe—without the half-hour wait—is a testament to how good it is. From 6am every day, you can get a big platter of pancakes or French toast for all of $4, or an over-stuffed omelet for $5. Post-brunch dessert? Why not reward yourself—Magnolia Bakery is right across the street.

Cabana Carioca
123 W. 45th St. (@ 7th Ave.)
Midtown 212.581.8088

Only in a very dire market can inflation go backwards. The all-you-can-eat first-floor lunch at this institution used to be $10.95; two years later it's plummeted $1 to the century's all-time low of $9.95. But rather than let it worry you, come and make merry. There are over 20 items on the buffet line masquerading as Brazilian but most are really just simple, rustic food. The protein-heavy dishes include a potato and salt cod casserole, roast chicken, and feijoada—the indigenous black bean stew, which falls thankfully short of being studded with parts of an entire pig. Who says it's a classless society? On the third floor, a more limited buffet goes for $5.95.

CAFÉ ASEAN
117 W. 10th St. (Greenwich & 6th Aves.)
West Village 212.633.0348

What a lunch spot! Count yourself lucky if the spider's web of West Village streets reels you into Café Asean, a rustic, cozy room serving Southeast Asian food so finely balanced as to allow "hearty" and "delicate" to co-exist. The Vietnamese, Malaysian, and Thai dishes—which rarely top $10—sing out with flavor and moistness. But—thanks to the worldly sensibilities of Malaysian-born chef Simpson Wong, who also owns next door's global restaurant, Jefferson—they also steer clear of cliché. Thus, pork chops bathe in a honey marinade; curries are abundant with vegetables straight from the greenmarket; the summer roll brims with crisp greens and a surprise: roast duck.

CAFÉ GIGI
417 E. 9th St. (1st Ave. & Ave. A)
East Village 212.505.3341

If you're a late riser and sick of taking flack for it, starting with the way McDonald's ends breakfast at 11am, then you'll be in good company at Café Gigi. This unapologetic bohemian den doesn't even open until 10am, and a seriously cheap breakfast is served 'til 4pm every day. Two eggs any way with toast and home fries are all of $3.25; add a quarter and get bacon or sausage with that. Omelets start at $4, and the weekend brunch—complete with salad and coffee or orange juice—doesn't top $8.50. Then it's waking-up food: quiche ($6), crispy thin-crust rounds of pizza ($7 and up), $1 BYOB corkage...until 2am. With these prices, need I mention where Ronald can stick his McMuffins?

CORNER BISTRO
331 W. 4th St. (@ Jane St.)
West Village 212.242.9502

Sure, this spot is plenty overexposed. But it's not like the no-ambiance café a few notches short of a diner has a great publicist. Its eight-oz. Bistro Burgers are really that good. For $6, you get a juicy round of meat slightly bigger than the bun, piled high with fresh tomatoes, melted cheese, and bacon, served on a paper plate. McSorley's is $2 and the place stays open 'til 4am.

FLOR DE MAYO
2651 Broadway (100th & 101st Sts.)
Upper West Side 212.663.5520

Cuban Chinese joints are fast disappearing, to the disappointment of people who know that some of the best Latino food in the city is cooked by descendents of Asian expats on Castro's island. But lucky for us, this part-Cuban Chinese, part-Peruvian Chinese (two partners, two mixed heritages) spot remains. Rotisserie chicken is what you want, and rotisserie chicken you shall have, with rice or plantains on the side. For $6.75 you get a half of a moist, tender chicken adorned with tickly, Peruvian spices. You'll never go back to KFC.

FRIED DUMPLING
99 Allen St. (@ Delancey St.)
Lower East Side 212.941.9975

If you didn't know where to find it, you'd never be able to pluck this tiny storefront out among the gaggle of Chinese signs choking the corner. The nondescript list of offerings on the window makes the place look like a copy shop, but once you're in, the unmistakable sound of frying—accompanied by the lovely smell of pork and soy sauce—dispel all notions of Xeroxes. Fried dumplings—made fresh in the back by a squadron of women—are only five for $1, as are the dainty little pan-fried pork buns. Skip the watery soybean drink, but ask about the day's selection (I recommend the pork with pungent Chinese chives), and pick up a 50-cent wedge of sesame bread with your order. You'll get change back from a $5 bill and wish you knew about this place sooner. Too bad they don't cater.

JOE'S PIZZA
233 Bleecker St. (@ Carmine St.)
West Village 212.366.1182

In a city packed with pizza by the slice, Joe's is a joint you actually want to go out of your way for. For $2.25, you get a thin slice of dripping hot pizza, topped with tangy, sweet tomato sauce and patches of fresh mozzarella. None of the plastic-y, reheated stuff here: Pies are made to order. With these lines, they go fast, so the supply is being constantly replenished. Ambiance is the only drawback: You must stand while ingesting, but share your cold winter's day with a couple of hot ovens; who's complaining?

L'ECOLE
462 Broadway (@ Grand St.)
SoHo 212.219.3300

The French Culinary Institute was founded to teach budding chefs how to cook the kind of dishes that use French techniques, fresh American ingredients, and ethnic twists, resulting in the contemporary cuisine that commands $20+ per entrée in any self-respecting three-star restaurant. The much-respected school conducts a program in which senior-level students prepare complex meals. Here's where you stand to benefit: Under the supervision of the instructors, the students at the school labor day and night at its hands-on restaurant, L'Ecole. It's like Restaurant Week all year long, since diners pay $20.04 for a three-course lunch and $29.95 for a four- or five-course dinner. The seasonal menus change every six weeks.

POPEYE'S CHICKEN AND BISCUITS

Manhattan Locations
Harlem: 2730 Frederick Douglass Blvd. (@ 145th St.) • 53 W. 116th St. (Lenox & 5th Aves.)
Midtown: 1558 3rd Ave. (57th & 58th Sts.) 722 7th Ave. (@ 49th St.) • 53 W. 46th St. (5th & 6th Aves.) • 221 W. 34th St. (7th & 8th Aves.)
Gramercy : 75 Lexington Ave. (@ 26th St.)
Flatiron: 47 W. 14th St. (5th & 6th Aves.)
East Village: 214 1st Ave. (11th & 12th Sts.)
Financial District: 112 Chambers St. (Church St. & W. Broadway) • 143 Fulton St. (Broadway & Nassau Sts.)
Chinatown: 52 Bowery St. (@ Canal St.)
For a complete list of locations in other boroughs, go to www.popeyes.com

This is the one exception to the no-fast-food rule of this book, but Popeye's is so good I couldn't resist. When the lines are long and the food is cheap, it's almost possible to believe we're living in simpler times, where no one's ever heard of the words "partially hydrogenated" and TV dinners are a treat. If you've sworn off fried food you're losing out:

Crispy and juicy chicken are the draws to this joint. I go for the biscuits—soft and misshapen pats of hot, butter-touched dough. For an extra deal, look for coupons online or in the Sunday paper.

SCHILLER'S LIQUOR BAR
131 Rivington St. (@ Norfolk St.)
Lower East Side 212.260.4555

Use this new bohemian den to sample Keith McNally's much-lauded restaurant know-how (he owns Balthazar and Pastis), but for way less moolah. Distressed mirrors and subway-tiled walls complement the checked floor and worn, mismatched tables. Most of the hip, comfort-oriented brunch (weekends only), lunch, and dinner menus (think fried oyster po' boys) goes for under $20. A chopped liver mousse dotted with caramelized onions? It's not your momma's, but the filling stuff is only $8. If you're opting for liquor of the grape variety, glasses of wine range from $5-$7, and a half-carafe is $8-$10. Cake, cinnamon, and powdered-sugar donuts—moister than the ones from your local coffee cart, less sugary than Krispy Kremes—are just $1 during lunch and brunch. At brunch, Schiller's pipes in classical tunes and puts out copies of the *Times*. One glance at the bar and you know that your Bloody Mary is in good hands.

SPICE
60 University Pl. (@ 10th St.)
Greenwich Village 212.982.3758

199 8th Ave. (20th & 21st Sts.)
Chelsea 212.989.1116

1411 2nd Ave. (73rd & 74th Sts.)
Upper East Side 212.988.5348

Surprised? So was I. I mean, this spot is a chain—although it's only gotten that way on the stilts of its own popularity. And authentic? The pad thai comes on a plate in a mold, for chrissake. These concerns aside, lunch here is phenomenal. Most dishes have a prix fixe price tag of $6-$8, including a fusion appetizer (so what if a summer roll dipped in plum sauce is downright gimmicky—and not at all Thai). The ambiance is clean and modern, the harried service is at least friendly, and the main portions are gigantic. You'll walk away patting your belly, which you could swear was taut when you walked in.

WONG WAH BAKERY
83 Canal St. (Eldridge & Allen Sts.)
Chinatown 212.343.8777

It's no small feat to be the Chinatown bakery with the perfect score from the health department. Top that achievement with warm, fresh goods—if you're lucky enough to get to them before they sell out. The selection has none of the neon-iced, plastic-looking nonsense in other C-town bake shops. In their place is a row of fresh, soft, sugar-topped rolls, called "pineapple" buns for the look, not the taste. The bakery also has squishy rice cakes filled with sweet bean paste, and hot dogs baked in either a sweet bun (a sweet and salty, Chinese variation on pigs-in-a-blanket) or in a compartment studded with pungent, Chinese chives. Prices are standard—at 40 or 50 cents, that roll is a pagoda or two better than your stale coffee cart kaiser.

YI MEI GOURMET FOOD INC.
51 Division St. (@ Market St.)
Chinatown 212.925.1921

7am is when the doors open at this street vendor-like Chinatown shop—which means the cooks get in at 5 to prepare for a busy day dispensing endless mounds of fresh-cooked Chinese food. Customers—largely Chinese men dotted with Latinos who can tell a good stir-fry—pile in for the unbelievable bargain: a choice of four items from the buffet, plus a bowl of rice, and egg drop soup for $2.75. If this sounds too heavy for breakfast, get a look at the pancake-sized fried eggs, fresh fried crullers (like unsweetened churros), and eggs hard-boiled in a tea-soy marinade. Moving on, get your day's supply of C and Z with narrow breaded strips of whole trout, strips of seaweed salad, pale green crescents of stir-fried bitter melon, and the juicy, chopped, soy-stewed chicken.

3 MOTOR CHEAP

Planes, trains, and automobiles can figure heavily into a NYC budget, especially if the city starts getting to you faster than carbon monoxide through a wind tunnel. Here are some ways—including inter-city, intra-city, and bushman-type journeys—to cut your travel costs to a bare-bones minimum.

CHINATOWN BUS SERVICE

In the realm of not-so-ancient Chinese secrets, here's a cool one: For next to nada, you can ride between northeastern Chinatowns in the comfort of a heated and air-conditioned mini-van. There are several bus services, and by no means is everyone on there going to be shouting angry-sounding Cantonese. A one-way to Philadelphia costs as little as $12, one-way from New York to Boston: $10, one-way to Washington, D.C.: $20, and one-way to Providence, R.I.: $25.

TODAY TRAVEL
39 E. Broadway (Forsyth & Market Sts.)
Chinatown 212.964.6334

FUNG WAH BUS TRANSPORTATION INC
139 Canal St., 1st Fl. (@ Forsyth St.)
Chinatown 212.925.8999

JET BLUE AIRLINES

The color blue stealthily, abruptly, and perhaps rightfully became the coolest color in the city. A stream of blues—Blue Water Grill, Blue Hill, Blue Smoke (all restaurants)—have steadily materialized on the Hudson horizon, followed, with much fanfare, by the airline Jet Blue. Taking a cue from the West Coast's wildly successful Southwest Airlines, there are some similarities: The fares are cheap, the vibe casual, and it's possible to buy a one-way segment and fly to secondary airports, such as Long Beach and Ontario rather than LAX. But our boy blue goes even further: The seats are assigned, and they are—in plush leather—luxurious, facing monitors that pipe in real-time television. JFK is the hub, with flights heading for many ports west, southwest, and south. To Florida alone there are a whopping five destinations: The airline knows where its bread is buttered. Some sample fares: a round-trip to Seattle for $238, or to Puerto Rico for $158.

MTA

Here's an idea: Timeshare your unlimited-use MetroCard. It's totally permissible: there's no clause that says you can't transfer the card to another holder. What other city gives you a free trip for buying a $10 MetroCard? Bus-subway transfers are also free. And there's a tax-free purchase option called TransitChek if your employer is hip to it: It allows you to buy a MetroCard with your stronger dollar, or pre-tax income. Sing along with me, "I want my...I want my...I want my MTA." Free transfers are electronically stored on your MetroCard.

GETTING TO THE AIRPORT

For basic Manhattan entries and exits, Olympia Airport Express can run you to and from Newark Liberty International Airport from the Port Authority terminal, Penn Station, or Grand Central Station for $12 each way ($19 round trip). The bus runs every 15 to 30 minutes from 4am to midnight. AirTrain is a different beast: The new airport service that links PATH, New Jersey Transit, and Amtrak rail riders to Newark Airport runs one-three trains an hour. The advantage is getting a cheap ride to a wider selection of destinations, including points in New Jersey, Midtown Manhattan, and the Wall Street area. Disadvantage: switching trains with all that luggage. Just take whatever train you're taking to the shiny new Rail Link station at Newark Airport, and the AirTrain whisks you right to the airport terminals for anywhere from $8-$13 one-way.

The options to and from LaGuardia and JFK are simpler. The New York Airport Service Express Bus charges $10-$13 for a one-way fare from Penn Station, Grand Central, or Port Authority.

AirTrain 973.762.5100

New York Airport Service Express Bus 718.875.8200

Olympia Airport Express 212.964.6233

STATEN ISLAND FERRY

Before your nose tilts skyward, stop right there: What has Staten Island ever done to you? Right; not a thing to deserve its shameful, outcast scarlet S. This falsely accused outpost is in fact home to lush greenery, rolling hills, friendly people, old mansions, shipyards, a few great pizzerias, and the kind of eyeful you get whenever you've just left Manhattan. Within walking distance to the ferry is the Snug Harbor Cultural Center, a gaggle of stunning Greek revival mansions in a watery oasis of calm and order. The ferry itself is like traveling third-class on a massive, crusty old cruise liner: commuters sitting side by side with, well, other commuters, and you.

STA TRAVEL
10 Downing St. (Bleecker & Houston Sts.)
West Village 212.627.3111

2871 Broadway (111th & 112th Sts.)
Upper West Side 212.865.2700

30 3rd Ave. (9th & 10th Sts.)
East Village 212.473.6100

254 Greene St. (E. 8th St. & Waverly Pl.)
Greenwich Village 212.254.2525

205 E. 42nd St. (2nd & 3rd Aves.)
Midtown 212.822.2700

Aren't you one lucky SOB? In college, you backpacked your way through Europe on a shoestring budget so skinny a mouse could have flossed his teeth with it. Just because you've graduated to an income (did you say rat floss?) is no reason not to relive your promiscuous, hard-drinking holidays

(What? You never left them?). Maybe you'll pack a suitcase this time, instead of that 100-lb. nylon number you ran with to catch the last train out of Prague, and book hotels where you don't have to BYOS (bring your own sheets). In any case, STA Travel is not just for the under-26ers in their seventh year of undergrad: The student's travel agency is offering an increasing number of discount fares to the over-26ers, not to mention the way-over-26ers. Oh, don't worry, STA still rewards people enrolled in degree programs (even part time) with cheap regular sabbaticals they don't deserve. But get out your passport: You non-academics can fly to London for as little as $210 round trip on Kuwait Airlines. Have an urge for a real caipirinha? Varig will deliver you to Sao Paolo and back, with a stopover in Rio, for $529. Ongoing domestic fares are available on ATA, like the $239 that gets you to LA and back.

OWNING A CAR
IN MANHATTAN

Okay, so you say, I bought this book, so I don't have money for a car. But miraculously, some of us poor New Yorkers do have cars, and suffer willingly through the nightmares of parking them, sitting in traffic, and paying for tolls, fuel, and insurance. (I know of a native Californian who drives daily from the Upper West Side to her downtown office.) If you're driving to either of the Queens airports or the Hamptons, you can avoid the toll at the Queens-Midtown Tunnel by taking the Queensboro Bridge (also known as the 59th St. Bridge) to the toll-free Long Island Expressway (I-495). Similarly, the toll-free Williamsburg Bridge or Manhattan Bridge will both shoot you onto Route 278 North, which in turn will take you to the L.I.E.

And when you're tearing your hair out, an hour late to yet another cancelled doctor's appointment, consider just getting a bicycle.

EDISON PARK FAST
Various locations in Manhattan, Brooklyn & New Jersey 877.727.5327

Don't call this a garage; it's car storage. Think of it as a coat check where you can only get your coat once a week, and pay a $5 tip every time. At 33rd & 9th, you'll typically pay $160/month, but sales do happen and recently rates were as low as

$127/month at 245–251 W. 28th St. (7th & 8th Aves.), 272–276 Spring St. (@ Varick St.), and 713–719 10th Ave. (48th & 49th Sts.). But move quickly: The bargain spots fill up within weeks.

I don't care how tiny your apartment is; sooner or later you're going to want to throw a classy kind of shindig. Sure, you can cater the event, but why go to the expense? I'm personally inspired by the girlfriend who cooked a Korean dinner party for 16 in a kitchen with two burners, a broiler with a broken door, and standing room for exactly one person—using a fold-up ironing board as a countertop. If she can do it, what's your excuse?

HERE ARE SOME IDEAS FOR CUTTING THE COSTS.

BEST CELLARS
1291 Lexington Ave. (86th & 87th Sts.)
Upper East Side 212.426.4200

Employees refer to this store as the "BC Mother Ship" for being the original and biggest of a burgeoning chain. But don't worry, none of the wines come from outer space. Astoundingly, the thousands of bottles stocking the shelves sell for $15 and less: Owners bypass larger producers, whose higher prices often reflect the costs of marketing and advertising. You benefit from the incredible bargains, topped with recommendations by a knowledgeable staff.

You'll find a thorough selection that represents small-scale production the world over, with even emphasis on Old World standbys, New World discoveries, and even up-and-coming vintages from New York State. Regular fun can be had in the themed nightly tastings. The staff selects one wine from the wall to support a chosen weekly theme (i.e., celebrating Earth Day, or Back to School). The wine is served from 5pm-8pm Monday-Friday. Saturdays from 2pm-4pm the fun expands, with a guest chef preparing food to pair with the samplings.

NOTE: This is a rare wine shop willing to exchange bottles that are corked, or have gone off because of a bad cork.

DAVE AND TONY'S SALUMERIA
35-18 30th Ave. (@ 35th St.)
Astoria 718.728.4850

This place beats Little Italy hands down as a source for odd shaped, imported pastas—the selection is wider and the prices lower. D&Ts also draws cured meat connoisseurs: It's $10/lb. for the domestic Prosciutto di Parma, and $17 for the imported kind. To round out your Italian meal, check out the homemade mozzarella, $4.99/lb., and a rich hunk of Parmigiano Reggiano for $12/lb.

EAST VILLAGE CHEESES
40 3rd Ave. (9th & 10th Sts.)
East Village 212.477.2601

It's more than a little ironic. Murray's Cheese Shop, the long-time Greenwich Village cheese retailer, is indirectly responsible for the success of its newer, cross-town rival. True, Murray Greenberg didn't give his fateful advice until after he sold his famous retail shop, but East Village Cheeses owners

Al and Carol Kaufman wisely took it to heart. The formula: Buy the surplus cheese from wholesalers, then pass the savings on to consumers. Over two successful decades later, the imported cheese shop does give off the discount aura of a surplus shop, the Odd-Lot of the dairy industry. You can't even see through the front window, it's so papered with the frenetic, red-marker-and-exclamation-points pricing of specials, as in: Wedges of double-cream brie for $1.50!! Ricotta fresca for $3/lb!!!! The knowledgeable staff can't be friendlier, although they also can't give you any tastings (see the sign in all caps). Cast your eyes up to the blackboard above the counter for the daily $2.99/lb. specials: mild Dutch goudas, pungent Rocqueforts, grassy Manchegos, civilized Gloucesters. Nothing tops more than $8 or $9 a pound if it's extra-special (extra-aged, perhaps). And the store—thanks to the varied products of wholesalers—isn't only about cheese: A 250-gram block of European sweet cream butter is only $2, a round of Boursin $1.50 (normally $6), and roasted whole coffee beans are $1-$2 less than you'd pay at Starbucks. For cheese, a half-pound minimum is in effect, and the store accepts cash only on all purchases.

ECONOMY CANDY
108 Rivington St. (Ludlow & Essex Sts.)
Lower East Side 212.254.1531

Is it a Halloween party? In 60-odd years, you better believe Economy's longtime owners have got their formula down. The result is a cram-packed shop bursting with insanely fresh candy from the cathedral-height rafters on down. Owner Jerry Cohen (and his father before him) has been sweetening his candy connections since 1937, bringing the benefits—and the closeouts—your way. Sample this: 75-cent sculpted mallow pops, old-fashioned candy sticks for 15 cents each,

$1.60 imported bars of Ritter Sport, $2/lb. of bright papaya spears, $4-$5/lb. for fat California pistachios, and $14.95 for an 18.6 oz. gift box of Ferrero Rocher. Wanna splurge? Go nuts with a giant Kermit the Frog pez dispenser for $18. Your sweet tooth—and your dentist—will thank you.

FAIRWAY SUPERMARKET
2127 Broadway (74th & 75th Sts.)
Upper West Side 212.595.1888

You have a two-hour window: Go. OK, so buying the after-hours goods at Fairway isn't as dramatic as winning a time-trial shopping spree at Macy's, but at least you'll end up with lunch(es). From 11pm-closing time (1am), the slashed goodies are pre-wrapped gourmet sandwiches and baked goods (loaves, rolls) for as much as 50% off (it's $2.50 for a sandwich that may have cost $5.50 for your big-spending counterpart at noon).

FLAIR BEVERAGE
3857 9th Ave. (@ 207th St.)
Inwood 212.569.8713

Spanning three city blocks, this yawning warehouse is beer and soda central. Prices for kegs date back to 1988: Coors is $40, Bud Light $50 (plus $10 keg deposit). Too sophisticated for kegs, you say? You can also get cases of everything from Corona and Heineken to Guinness and Anchor Steam, starting from $20 for 24 bottles. While you're at it, score some for the expectant moms in your circle of friends: Eight 2-liter bottles of soda (pretty much anything in the commercial soda brand universe) costs not much more than $8. Donate some of your savings to the cab drivers fund; unfortunately, Flair doesn't deliver.

JACK'S 99 CENT STORE
110 W. 32nd St. (@ 6th Ave.)
Midtown 212.268.9962

The Bloomingdale's of dollar stores, Jack's isn't your usual 99-cent shopping. Its goods are splayed on multiple floors and organized into separate departments. Upstairs you'll find closeout items at bargain basement prices: Toys, appliances, and designer boxes of chocolate proliferate. Downstairs, everything is truly just a dollar, including housewares (Tupperware-like containers, ceramic bowls), hardware (tools, flashlights), personal goods (electric toothbrushes, soap), more toys (puzzles, dolls), seasonal paraphernalia (Christmas lights, wrapping paper), office and cleaning supplies, and food. The latter is where you can consistently score biggest; you'll see items you bought yesterday at your local super-market for $3.49 at the magic price, including cold cuts, eggs, and milk.

KASHKAVAL
856 9th Ave. (55th & 56th Sts.)
Hell's Kitchen 212.581.8282

Waltz right past the cheesy $1.99 cheeses (low-fat American? C'mon!) and proceed directly to the aromatic sacks of whole plain and flavored coffee beans. For after-dinner treats, they're only $5.99/lb.—a substantial savings over Starbucks. Cherry! Mmmm.

KEY FOOD
52 Ave. A (@ E. 4th St.)
East Village 212.477.9063

Prices so low, aisles so wide: You'll think you've taken the F train and gone to Westchester…until you spot plantains in the pro-duce section and herring salad in the deli case and realize you haven't left Manhattan. Despite the wide format, the supermarket isn't quite full-service; there are five kinds of olives in the thoroughly stocked deli case, but there's neither butcher nor baker on-site. Still, the prices are insanely cheap, particularly the daily specials. Spotted: fresh whole Perdue roasters for 79 cents/lb., a 96-oz. container of Tropicana for $2.74, six Yoplait yogurts for $3, and my personal favorite, a 5-lb. bag of kitty litter for 99 cents. Meowsers.

MEDITERRANEAN FOODS
30-12 34th St. (@ 30th Ave.)
Astoria 718.728.6166

23-18 31st St. (23rd & 24th Aves.)
Astoria 718.721.0221

The smell of olives smacks into you like a fast-moving racquetball knocking into a baby carriage. Small wonder: An olive bar sits in the middle of this clean, bright 34th Street shop; that's 30 varieties recycling the air from their open jars like a powerful ocean breeze. It's possible to come away from this 30-year-old Greek specialty store with a three-liter tin of extra virgin olive oil for the rock-bottom price of $10.55, a 32-oz. jar of fat, imported capers for $3, a pound of Prosciutto di Parma for $10, and a huge container of fresh Turkish delight (called Greek delight here, of course) for less than $5. Although the man behind the cheese counter may not understand a word you are saying (but still nod as if he did), cheeses are a good find, too: The best feta is a creamy imported variety that tastes nothing like the domestic salt mine, and the pliable, store-made mozzarella is only $4.25/lb. The store even sells Greek soap. Representing the best of the Old World, this place has a few New World conveniences: It's open long hours (from 8am-9pm most days), sells in bulk, has air conditioning, and takes credit cards.

SOHO FRUIT & VEGETABLE STAND
SE corner of Broadway & Houston St.
SoHo

This seasonal godsend sells more than fruit in a setup that's resolutely more than a stand. Almost everything costs $1.50; among the best buys are the garlic (four fat heads), ginger (a giant's handful), Red Delicious apples (six), and gorgeous red bell peppers (another quartet). Enjoy it while it's there: open May to October only.

UNION SQUARE GREENMARKET
Union Square (E. 17th St. & Broadway)
Mondays, Wednesdays, Fridays, and
Saturdays
Flatiron

Fresher food at better prices—so what's the catch? True, not all the products in this chef's paradise are a cut-rate bargain (e.g. the $6 jars of honey and jam), but a wander amongst the farmerly bins makes it obvious what is: lettuce so fresh you can smell it, beets and potatoes in a rainbow of colors and patterns, a garden's harvest of potent herbs. Top that with the abundant sampling and the farmer-friendly 'tude (especially on Fridays, when the stalls are fullest), and soon they'll have to stage an intervention plan, since the only catch is the addiction.

GETTING HITCHED -
FOR CHEAP

Of all the weddings in all the cities in the world...who is really going to remember yours? Even if you really want your wedding to be chatter fodder for years to come, there is no golden rule that chains a string of dollar signs to the concept: One bride I know of made a splash at her wedding by spewing champagne into her dinner.

On a brighter note, a resourceful couple I know saved money—and added special touches—at their wedding when the bride made her own invitations, then asked a former colleague to officiate in a public park, her talented college roommate to sing both processional and recessional, her cousin to cater, another cousin to bartend, and her brother to deejay. Her lovely antique ivory silk dress came from her mother's vintage closet. The groom's mother cooked the rehearsal dinner, and his sister emceed a portion of the reception. The personal touches upped the sentimental ante...and the couple used their savings for new furniture in their Brooklyn apartment.

There are still plenty of ways to save money if you have less talented friends and relatives and/or don't want to put them to work. Here are a few ideas.

HAVE YOUR CEREMONY AT CITY HALL.
Cost: $50

CITY HALL
1 Centre St. (@ Chambers St.)
TriBeCa 212.669.2400

Down to earth, yes. Boring? Oh, nooooo. Nobody said that just because you don't spend hundreds of dollars on an officiant, flowers, and venue, your City Hall ceremony has to be plain Jane. Feel free to show up at the building in matching turquoise outfits, trailed by an entourage. It's $25 for the permit and another $25 for the ceremony.

MAKE YOUR OWN INVITATIONS AND THANK YOU CARDS.
Cost: Materials

KATE'S PAPERIE
561 Broadway (@ Prince St.)
SoHo 212.941.9816

8 W. 13th St. (5th & 6th Aves.)
Greenwich Village 212.633.0570

1282 3rd Ave. (73rd & 74th Sts.)
Upper East Side 212.396.3670

140 W. 57th St. (6th & 7th Aves.)
Midtown 212.459.0700

Forget about that time you set fire to the Christmas cookies—this is different...you're getting married. Sure, love is no cure-all, but you can't go too far astray with a hands-on instructor telling you where to glue and fold. And think of the end product: personalized, memorable wedding invitations—and more money stashed away towards a love nest of your very own.

Twice a year, Kate's (see Learn Cheap) holds two wedding events—one in January and one in June. Don't have the knack? Then come for a slice of celebrity baker Martin Howard's wedding cake.

LEARN HOW TO DO YOUR OWN MAKEUP.
Cost: Free

SHISEIDO STUDIO
155 Spring St.
(W. Broadway & Wooster St.)
SoHo 212.625.8820

As any theater makeup person can tell you, the trick to doing a good job on special occasion makeup has everything to do with special effects. Highlighting the depth of your cheekbones while widening your eyes is generally not something you should try at home. But this studio offers beauty courses to bridal parties (preferably 10 or more) for absolutely free. They're hoping your entourage will convert to all Shiseido all the time. The good news? You won't get a dirty look if you don't buy—buying is by request only.

BUY YOUR DRESS AT THE ONCE-A-YEAR FILENE'S BASEMENT SALE.
Cost: $250-$500.

FILENE'S BASEMENT
620 6th Ave. (18th & 19th Sts.)
Chelsea 212.620.3100

2222 Broadway (@ 79th St.)
Upper West Side 212.873.8000

Brides-to-be can no longer have Filene's Basement envy. The famed day-long wedding-gown sale now comes to NYC. In August 2003, the event lived up to every bit of hype from Boston—brides and their entourages that had driven in from Long Island at 2am, a wraparound line an hour prior, a mad rush at the door to strip the metal racks bare of all dresses, and customers in bad '80s spandex with clothespins protruding in every direction. Brides come away with $250 gowns which retail for $2,000, or $500 designer gowns (Carolina Herrera, etc.) which retail for $4,000-$5,000. Sound like a freak show? You bet.

MAKING FRIENDS ON THE CHEAP

We are a city that loves our pets. Need proof? Look at all the dog shit. Or the dog walkers getting rich off of pet parents whose schedules manage to be somehow crazy and lazy all at once. This is one area of the economy that's proven to be recession-proof.

When purebred animals are selling for upwards of $1,000 each, the least expensive—and most responsible—place to adopt is the animal shelter. You don't necessarily have to give up your dream breed: The city's biggest shelter, the Center for Animal Care and Control, estimates that a third of the total number of animals (an eye-popping 1,000 dogs and cats) is purebred. The CACC, which charges a $35-$150 adoption fee (shots, neutering, and microchip included), has branches in all five boroughs. As an alternative, try the lesser-known Bide-a-Wee shelter, where adoptions are technically free. For Rover's sake, fork over the small, suggested fee of $30 ($55 for kittens and puppies).

CENTER FOR ANIMAL CARE AND CONTROL
326 E. 110th St. (1st & 2nd Aves.)
Upper East Side 212.722.3620

464 E. Fordham Rd. (@ 190th St.)
Bronx 718.733.0743

2336 Linden Blvd. (Essex St. & Shelter Ave.)
Brooklyn 718.272.7200

92-29 Queens Blvd. (Eliot & 62nd Aves.)
Rego Park 718.997.6330

3139 Veterans Rd. W. (@ Arthur Kill Rd.)
Staten Island 718.984.6643

BIDE-A-WEE
410 E. 38th St. (1st Ave. & FDR Dr.)
Murray Hill 212.532.4455

Could be your computer is inconveniently ensconced in an acorn of a studio on the waaaay Upper West Side, where you do little else but rest your city-addled head. Or you're just too cheap—or poor—to shell out $50 a month for high-speed Internet service (or worse, it goes down so often you cancelled it). Or you're one of those people who must check their e-mail every hour, on the hour (speaking from experience). The good news is the city is teeming with support centers for people like us.

Internet cafes are popping up all over town, and the competition is driving prices down and/or out. **The Three Jewels Café** (211 E. 5th St. @ 4th Ave.) will give you free broadband in exchange for a chance to promote their spiritual offerings—don't worry, all you need do is respect the spirit of the place and put a few dollars in the donation basket. In SoHo, banks of Apple's see-through computers await use at the **Apple Store** (103 Prince St. bet. Mercer & Greene Sts.). Chinatown, Little Tokyo, Koreatown, and the Lower East Side are rife with inexpensive computer banks used by gaming teenagers late into the night…but available for the average schmo during the quiet days. Hotel lobbies can be a good bet, too, so long as you play things cool. For example, non-guests are able to use the Sony Vaio in the lobby of the **W Hotel** in Murray Hill (E. 39th St. @ Lexington Ave.).

Uptown, **Café Mozart** (154 W. 70th St. @ Broadway) offers free access for any schmo buying a pastry and a cup of coffee. Then there's always the closest branch of the **New York Public Library**, but use those as last resorts: Wait lists are common and can be long.

If you have a laptop with an internal or external wireless network card, things get even easier. Pockets of the city have achieved new heights of WiFi savvy, providing you with free hubs of varying signal strength. Check out **Bryant Park** (40th & 42nd Sts., 5th & 6th Aves.), where you can sit for hours under the shade in nice weather. Downtown, **Bowling Green** (@ the foot of Broadway), **City Hall Park** (Broadway & Park Row), and **Union Square Park** (4th Ave. & Broadway, 14th & 17th Sts.) all provide steady outdoor access. Indoor access can be had in the food court at Pier 17, the mall by the **South Street Seaport** (Water St. to the East River bet. Dover & Fletcher Sts.), in the living room-like ambiance of **alt.coffee** (139 Ave. A), and pretty much anywhere within **Chelsea Market** (75 9th Ave. @ W. 16th St.). And far uptown, check out **DTUT Café** (1626 2nd Ave. @ 84th St.), which charges $2 an hour, but in return, you get cozy antique ambiance and no pointed glares from the wait staff. In Brooklyn, check out the garden at the **Brooklyn Museum** (200 Eastern Pkwy.).

To get a complete and up-to-date listing of free hotspots, visit www.nycwireless.net, a non-profit organization dedicated to assisting in the deployment of free wireless community networks throughout the NYC metro area.

Just for living in the world's most cultural city, you get constant, easy access to world-class events that recur as certainly as the reader on your electric meter. Most—although not all—of the following festivals happen in the luscious NYC summertime.

CELEBRATE BROOKLYN
Prospect Park Bandshell (Prospect Park West & 9th St.) Park Slope

Joan Armatrading was the opening headliner at 2003's Celebrate Brooklyn. That pretty much sums up this long-standing festival (2003 marked the 25th anniversary): gigs of astronomical value with a distinct, multicultural spice. Early in the summer, Celebrate Brooklyn gets a jump on the Canada Day celebration in Central Park, a few days before the actual birthday of our neighbor to the north with acts by Canadian artists, of which there are an astounding number (Sarah McLachlan, Rufus Wainwright).

NOTE: The entryway motto is: Keep it great! Give $3 at the gate! Pony up, will ya?

CENTRAL PARK'S SUMMERSTAGE
Rumsey Playfield (69th St. entrance off 5th Ave.) Central Park

The most popular and diverse free gathering in all of New York City happens on this modest semicircle of astro turf, beneath an unassuming bandshell. But don't underestimate the scene: The speakers have every bit of capacity to blow off your hat and maybe your clothes, too. SummerStage is a 25-year-old tradition. The 30-plus events—divided into spoken word, dance, and rocking American and world music—are mostly free, all except for a handful of self-benefit performances from crowd-pleasers like Devo. Shows go on rain or shine—on bright weekend days, arrive well before the 90-minute opening of the gates to claim a patch of your very own. If the music part of the fest delivers on its promise, it won't matter how tough the turf is—you'll be up and dancing in no time.

NOTE: You can't bring booze or coolers, but you can bring a backpack, and there are reasonably priced concession booths that flank the space.

EVENINGS AT THE PICTURE SHOW
Socrates Sculpture Park (@ Broadway & Vernon Blvd.) Long Island City 718.516.819

The folks in Queens have developed some awfully evocative names for their festivities. Here's one that only half describes what this September-long celebration—prolonging summer—is all about. The "picture show" does refer to the movies—mostly shorts—shown at sunset on Saturday evenings, but only following other free festivities including a live band and art workshops. If you're childless, keep in mind that there may be lots of little tykes running around: The MoMA has made extra-special effort to ensure that band lyrics stay "kid-friendly."

GOOD MORNING AMERICA SUMMER CONCERT SERIES
Bryant Park (40th & 42nd Sts., 5th & 6th Aves.) Midtown

There's nothing as bracing as a rock concert at 7am on a Friday morning. That's the hour you're going to be dressed, coiffed, and already in Bryant Park. Between Memorial Day and Labor Day, the magnanimous commercial talent arrives. Santana, Third Eye Blind, and Liz Phair have all mounted the outdoor stage at Bryant Park for their live ABC broadcast with Diane and Charlie. Never underestimate a caffeine-pumped New Yorker: The concerts fill up quickly, even for Phair, who performed without the use of electronics during Blackout 2003. Just remember to be at work in time for Friday's free donuts.

HARLEM MEER PERFORMANCE FESTIVAL
Charles A. Dana Discovery Center (110th St. bet. 5th & Lenox Aves.)
Harlem 212.860.1370

For something a little more smoldering, Sunday afternoons from May to September bring salsa, gospel, and jazz to this 11-acre lake in Central Park. The lakeshore in front of the Reader's Digest Plaza provides a glittering, woodsy ampitheatre, which adds to the aesthetic appeal of the gorgeous setting, if not the acoustics.

HOBOKEN ARTS & MUSIC FESTIVAL
Washington St. (Newark & 7th Sts.)
Hoboken 201.420.2207

When a tried and true Jersey town throws a party, it means business. A recent expansion to include four outdoor performance stages and rows upon rows of food and craft stalls means the twice-yearly festival draws 100,000 people per event. The music—which changes on each of the four stages every 45 minutes—is varied and good; you can expect a few singer-songwriters in the mix, along with great blues, jazz, alternative rock, Brazilian beat, and funk bands.

HOWL FESTIVAL
The Federation of East Village Artists
East Village 212.505.2225

This paean to Allen Ginsberg and his ilk is militant, forthright, and indignant. Counterculture began in the East Village, dammit, and the collective descent of yuppies and foodies cannot rub out the legacies of Charlie Parker, Emma Goldman, Keith Haring, Jean-Michel Basquiat, and The Ramones. HOWL is the lovechild, a new (as of 2003) annual summer festival started by FEVA, the Federation of East Village Artists, whose mission statement comes down to this: We stand on the shoulders of gods to fight for the rights of East Village artists. History isn't the only thing to endow this neighborhood: Venues span a rich and diverse gamut, from the Bowery Poetry Club, to the serenity of Tompkins Square Park, to the LES' Fusion Arts Museum, to the graceful lines of St. Mark's Church. In its first year, the festival encompassed all of the following: the Charlie Parker Jazz Festival, Art Around the Park, the Allen Ginsberg Poetry Festival, and the return of Wigstock.

LINCOLN CENTER OUT OF DOORS
Lincoln Center (W. 62md & 65th Sts.,
Columbus & Amsterdam Aves.)
Upper West Side 212.875.5000
www.lincolncenter.org

For more than 30 years, the plazas outside Lincoln Center have doubled as stages for this four-week summer festival. You'll find everything from Memphis blues and jazz to steel drums and modern dance, with every bit of the signature excellence to be expected.

ON THE WATERFRONT: CELEBRATING THE CULTURAL DIVERSITY OF QUEENS
Socrates Sculpture Park
(@ Broadway & Vernon Blvd.)
Long Island City 718.956.1819

It's a mouthful to say, but really, Queensites know this festival as good summer fun without having to climb on the 7 train. Music is free. Films are free. The skyline is glistening. The festival takes complete advantage of Queens' patchwork of ethnicities, one of which is chosen at each event to form a theme. An Italian theme translates to the lasagna of a local vendor, consumed picnic-style on the lawn of the Socrates Sculpture Park with *The Bicycle Thief* playing on the big outdoor screen. Ditto less familiar heritages—and bravo to Queens for saluting the Senegalese, Yugoslavian, and Brazilian cinema.

RIVER TO RIVER FESTIVAL
Various venues in downtown Manhattan

It's fitting that the hardest-working man in show business—soul king James Brown—should have kicked off New York City's most bountiful (measured by the sheer number of events) free festival in 2003. The River to River Festival, the cultural extravaganza that descends on our ever-stunning Financial District, itself represents a good union, with financial giant American Express as its primary sponsor. Aside from Brown, show headliners have included Friday night "sunset jams" and the popular Twyla Tharp Dance Company, but this festival—which takes full advantage of the triple blessing of Battery Park, the World Financial Center, and South Street Seaport—isn't just about performances. Events have included a white wine tasting and a candlelit walking tour of revolutionary monuments on the 4th of July.

@ the Hudson River (Battery Park to 59th St.)
Hudson River Park 212.791.2530

Whoever said New York was a treasure trove for outdoor lovers knew exactly what they were talking about. The Hudson River Park—not even complete yet—is every city's dream of a stolen greenspace: recaptured waterfront spanning 13 commercial piers handily converted for recreational use. Now, the asphalt strip between Battery Park and Riverside Park is lined with gardens, sunning lawns, dog runs, and toilets.

Year-round, this makes an ideal throughway, and many a jogger, cyclist, or skater can be found taking advantage of the five miles completely unimpeded by traffic lights, yellow cabs, or honking horns (although expect to breathe in a certain amount of exhaust nevertheless). And summer is when the park comes into full bloom, with films (Riverflicks), live music (Hudson River Rocks), an annual race of the world's best outrigger canoes, and other assorted treats.

And one of the most unexpected summer treats is a dance band, held at the aptly titled Moondance on Sunday nights starting July 4—show up with a dancing partner if you want to show off your steps. The park commissions a dance band (e.g., the swing band George Gee's Jump Jive and Wailers) to appear at Pier 25 every Sunday. You get a half-hour lesson at 6:30pm, and the bands come on at 7pm.

Union Square Park (4th Ave. & Broadway, 14th & 17th Sts.) Flatiron 212.460.1200

Funded in part by corporate giants such as Barnes & Noble and Verizon, the casual, 7-year-old Summer in the Square takes advantage of Union Square Park, where a makeshift outdoor stage faces a natural amphitheater (in other words, bring a blanket or sit on the grass). You can sit close enough to smell the sweat and spot the mosquito bites on a ballerina's legs. The events happen Wednesdays in a three-part lineup: live music, storytelling (don't forget Barnes & Noble's involvement), and dance. The specifics are a little more variable: Dancers and musicians come in all forms and disciplines, and storytelling could encompass anything from enactments of children's books to poetry. The setting is idyllic…except for the occasional ambulance or dump truck passing by on 14th Street. In the event of rain, performances are rescheduled to another Wednesday at a different time of day.

A YEAR IN PARADES

Forget being un-American: It would be unforgivably un-New Yorker not to show your spirit in a street parade or a dozen— particularly when the watching is free and the only real hazard is wasting all your film unintentionally on the big hairdo at two o'clock. Starting with the ultra-safe and magnificently televised **NEW YEAR'S EVE BALL DROP** at Times Square, these traditions draw locals and tourists from far and wide (if you're going to go, dress warmly and remember that restrooms are few and far between). By the time the crowds have gathered in Midtown, **FIRST NIGHT**, a five-borough rainbow of events including crafts fairs, performances, and food, has already kicked off at noon on the 31st.

Next in line is **CHINESE NEW YEAR**, which generally falls in February or late January, and never fails to be equal parts kitsch and worthy spectacle, what with the exotic drumming and dancing lions meandering up the narrow Chinatown streets. If you prefer your revelry early (11am), then the **ST. PATRICK'S DAY PARADE**, a straight shot up 5th Avenue from 44th to 86th Streets, is exactly your thing. A month later, the elegant avenue spiffs up with the **EASTER PARADE** on Easter Sunday, replete with flowers, rabbits, and large, elaborate women's hats.

June is rife with parades. Kick off summer

with a glimpse of the homemade floats on Coney Island at the **MERMAID DAY PARADE**, which features women and men in silver wigs, sequined fish tails, and green paint. Mid-month, the Financial District hosts the talented street performers at the well-named **BUSKERS FARE**— 'tis a pity so many of the performers are imported. And later in the month, the **GAY PRIDE PARADE** is to be distinguished from the related rallies and marches: In the former it would not be unusual for a 6' 5" drag queen with waist-deep décolletage to give you the finger for stepping on her long purple tutu. On July 4, **MACY'S FIREWORKS** explode in and around both South Street Seaport and Herald Square (look also for other fireworks along the Hudson River and near Roosevelt Island).

Come fall, you'll see stilted clowns and human condoms and other lasting images at the **HALLOWEEN PARADE**, which wanders up 6th Avenue from Spring Street to 23rd Street, and all but replaces urban trick-or-treating, at least in Manhattan. On the first Sunday of November, come out and applaud the grimacing runners at the **NEW YORK CITY MARATHON**—the most obvious place to join the madding crowd, of course, is on the way to the finish line on 1st Avenue off the Queensboro Bridge. And for a real thrill, don't wait for Thursday to view the **MACY'S THANKSGIVING PARADE**; camp out after midnight the night prior for a surreal, front-row view of the floats as they come from New Jersey through the Lincoln Tunnel.

A few weeks later, there's the televised holiday lighting of the chosen tree at **ROCKEFELLER CENTER CHRISTMAS**, accompanied by invocations and skating and music. And, although they're not parades, the queues waiting to see the intricate window displays outside NYC's superstores (Macy's, Bloomingdale's, Saks Fifth Avenue, Lord and Taylor) shares the same spectator vibe.

NYC vibrates with creative energy: It seems wherever you are is perpetually a stone's throw away from a great indie record shop, used book shop, performance venue, or other creative outlet, particularly in student-ridden neighborhoods such as both the East and West Village. All of this leads to the great number of bargains that can be had with more soul than any mall or Virgin Megastore can offer, and more immediate gratification than eBay or anything you can order online.

DISC-O-RAMA

Main Store: 186 W. 4th St. (Jones & Barrow Sts.) West Village 212.206.8417

Annex: 40 Union Sq. East (@ 16th St.) Flatiron 212.260.8616

Clearance Store: 146 W. 4th St. (@ 6th Ave.) West Village 212.477.9410

The sign in the front of each of these stores claims—perhaps rightfully—their standing as "New York's headquarters for compact discs." True or not, there are a lot of the round musicmakers in all three stores, and none of them are bootlegged; instead they're used, if gently. No upstanding used CD store would stock anything that was scratched, so you'll get a shiny round at perfect playing capacity for $1-$6. Both the main store and annex have a tendency to stock cheap box sets, and cassettes if you still own a tape player. New discs will cost you $10 across the board. Avoid the expensive imports.

GENERATION RECORDS
210 Thompson St. (W. 3rd & Bleecker Sts.) Greenwich Village 212.254.1100.

This crammed shop is another Village favorite, probably best-known for its ability to turn up rare live recordings, which are generally priced at $20 and up. More common used CDs are also in evidence, and plentiful. While you're in, check out the wide selection of bootleg CDs…and don't ruin it for the rest of us, so hush.

HOUSING WORKS USED BOOK CAFÉ
126 Crosby St. (@ Spring St.) SoHo 212.334.3324

Don't want to spend a fortune on books? Enter Housing Works. With the look of a grand library with its swirling staircase and 20-foot pillared ceilings, Housing Works gets to do much more than sell a pile of dog-eared books: It also hosts weddings and semi-annual shindigs thrown by the likes of the *New Yorker*. It turns out the merchandise—100% donated—is not so dog-eared after all…but the cheapest among you should still note that this place is so not all about the cash. Free readings—often by celebrity authors—happen almost nightly, turning the intimate café into a brainiac's fantasy venue—all in the midst of retail-crazed SoHo. Even if there is a reading going on, there are still plenty of overstuffed armchairs—on the balcony, the front of the store—for curling up.

KIM'S VIDEO AND MUSIC
2906 Broadway (@ 113th St.)
Upper West Side 212.864.5321

6 St Marks Pl. (2nd & 3rd Aves.)
East Village 212.598.9985

85 Ave. A (@ E. 5th St.)
East Village 212.529.3410

144 Bleecker St. (@ LaGuardia Pl.)
Greenwich Village 212.260.1010

Kim's is a headquarters for mediaheads everywhere, whether they're renting movies or buying movies and/or new and used music. The stores are friendly and unpretentious, and stock everything: establishment, avant-rock, indie, psychedelica, metal. The West Village location recently bit the dust, leaving behind four others. Let's make sure they're not endangered, too.

NYC LIQUIDATORS INC.
158 W. 27th St. (6th & 7th Aves.)
Chelsea 212.675.7400

It smells like a bootlegger's paradise, but take another whiff. $1 videos and $2.98 DVDs—many brand-new in boxes and shrink-wrap, often just-released—are 100% legitimate. This is a true liquidation warehouse that even has an authentic warehouse look. The long, basement-like showroom is crammed with stacks of shelves, and also boxes, clutter, and incomplete labels. But soon enough, a system emerges. It turns out there's a bigger, second room containing the business' bread and butter: what else? Porn—you can get the hard-core stuff for $2 per tape, $5 per DVD. Moviewise, other heavy hitters are karate flicks, horror, music documentaries, recent blockbusters, Spanish-language movies, and even arthouse fare (spotted: *Amelie* and *Far From Heaven*). As for music, the CDs tend towards rock, hip-hop, and reggae, although you can find pretty much anything for a top price of $13.98. Call to find out about $1 CD closeout sales—they happen often and last for months on end.

NORMANS CDS NO. 2
33 St. Marks Pl. (1st & 2nd Aves.)
East Village 212.253.6162

Owned by the son of Norman, this is not to be confused with Norman's No. 1, the older, larger used-CD shop at 67 Cooper Square. Norman's No. 2—which stocks a similar selection of rock, jazz, R&B, soundtracks, DVDs, and brand-new releases, most for $10 and less—might well be the cheapest of its kind on the block. In any case, Norman's is probably the friendliest, with a staff that helps with suggestions and is willing to play almost anything you request over the store's speakers.

ST. MARK'S SOUNDS
16 St. Marks Pl. (2nd & 3rd Aves.)
East Village 212.677.3444

20 St. Marks Pl. (2nd & 3rd Aves.)
East Village 212.677.2727

Alas, Sounds has discontinued their $2.99 CDs. But this St. Marks music shop—which always has great shopping ideas blaring overhead—still has one of the widest selections of used CDs anywhere in the city. Used discs sell for a mere $5-$9. The store also has new CDs for about $12, a decent import collection, and vinyl.